More Praise for *Share This!*

"Deanna Zandt has a techie's brain and an organizer's heart. With this book, she shows us definitively (and entertainingly too) how our personal stories can do more than fill out our consumer profile. Together, they say, we can change the world. Deanna shows us how we can come together in a whole new way, right now."

—Laura Flanders, host of GRITtv and GRITradio
and author of *Blue Grit*

"Greedheads and boneheads, arrogance and ignorance. Can everyday people buck the system? Yes! Zandt shows us how, and how to have fun doing it!"

—Jim Hightower, national radio commentator
and author of *Swim Against the Current*

"*Share This!* is the book I wish I had written. Zandt writes with incredible knowledge, easy humor, and profoundly touching stories. If ever you needed that nudge to convince you that the web has fundamentally changed the game and that your participation is an important part of it, this is the book. I'm recommending it to everyone I know."

—Tara Hunt, author of *The Whuffie Factor*

"Progressive media activist and 'geek grrl' Deanna Zandt has been surfing the social media wave practically from the start. Whether you're looking to get your feet wet or want to dive in, *Share This!* shows not only how networked media is changing society but how we all can join in and make the most of it to help change the world."

—Micah Sifry, cofounder, Personal Democracy
Forum, and Editor, TechPresident.com

"You've never read a book like this before. Embrace the new. Go for it. It just might change your life."

—Don Hazen, Executive Editor, AlterNet.org

"Sick of hearing about how social media is changing everything? Deanna Zandt knows what you mean—and yet she's found a way to transcend the cynicism and remind us that beneath the hype, something amazing is happening as we build our digital lives around what still matters most: relationships."

—Monika Bauerlein, Coeditor, *Mother Jones*

"*Share This!* is a book that everyone from tech novices to old hands will enjoy. Zandt hits just the right note with her accessible and witty prose—this book is bound to change the way you think about social networking." —Jessica Valenti, founder, Feministing.com, and author of *The Purity Myth*

"Deanna Zandt is completely tapped into the social media matrix. Every activist working in the digital space needs this book." —Latoya Peterson, Editor, Racialicious.com

"After my daughter explained Facebook to me, I joined. (And surprised many of my friends!)" —Rachael Zandt, Administrative Assistant, Columbian Financial Group, and mother, Deanna Zandt

"Zandt's book is like a celebrity cooking show...it breaks down the ingredients of social media successes into basic and easy-to-understand ingredients. You will finish reading this manual with the amazing feeling of 'I can do this!'" —Scott Goodstein, External Online Director, Obama for America, and founder, Revolution Messaging

"Deanna Zandt is one of the smartest, savviest, and sharpest observers of the new world, new media, and new ideas." —Robert Greenwald, President, Brave New Films

"With media, technology, and politics having essentially merged, all activists for justice need to update their attitudes and their skills. This book by social media maven Deanna Zandt has just the right mix of the why and the how to convince the skeptical and equip the fearful." —Rinku Sen, Executive Director, Applied Research Center, and coauthor of *The Accidental American*

"Deanna Zandt thinks big, arguing that social media won't just change how we talk but how we live. Part analysis, part guidebook, *Share This!* offers a creative, ambitious view of a truly organic political landscape hinted at, but never really pursued, by the new political establishment." —Ben Smith, Senior Political Writer, *Politico*

"*Share This!* combines common sense, technically savvy how-to, and a grasp of the way in which human beings and technology come together and sometimes apart. Deanna Zandt is a first-rate guide for the 22nd century." —Amy Bloom, author of *Where the God of Love Hangs Out* and *Away*

SHARE THIS!

· ·

How **You** Will Change the World
with Social Networking

Deanna Zandt

BK

Berrett–Koehler Publishers, Inc.
San Francisco
a BK Currents book

Berrett-Koehler Publishers, Inc.
235 Montgomery Street, Suite 650
San Francisco, CA 94104-2916
Tel: (415) 288-0260   Fax: (415) 362-2512   www.bkconnection.com

Ordering Information
Quantity sales. Special discounts are available on quantity purchases by corporations, associations, and others. For details, contact the "Special Sales Department" at the Berrett-Koehler address above.
Individual sales. Berrett-Koehler publications are available through most bookstores. They can also be ordered directly from Berrett-Koehler: Tel: (800) 929-2929; Fax: (802) 864-7626; www.bkconnection.com
Orders for college textbook/course adoption use. Please contact Berrett-Koehler: Tel: (800) 929-2929; Fax: (802) 864-7626.
Orders by U.S. trade bookstores and wholesalers. Please contact Ingram Publisher Services, Tel: (800) 509-4887; Fax: (800) 838-1149; E-mail: customer.service@ingram publisherservices.com; or visit www.ingrampublisherservices.com/Ordering for details about electronic ordering.

Berrett-Koehler and the BK logo are registered trademarks of Berrett-Koehler Publishers, Inc.

Printed in the United States of America.

Berrett-Koehler books are printed on long-lasting acid-free paper. When it is available, we choose paper that has been manufactured by environmentally responsible processes. These may include using trees grown in sustainable forests, incorporating recycled paper, minimizing chlorine in bleaching, or recycling the energy produced at the paper mill.

Library of Congress Cataloging-in-Publication Data
Zandt, Deanna.
    Share this! : how you will change the world with social networking / by Deanna Zandt. — 1st ed.
        p. cm.
    Includes bibliographical references and index.
    ISBN 978-1-60509-416-8 (paperbound : alk. paper)
1. Social networks. 2. Social networks—Political aspects. 3. Social media. I. Title.
    HM741.Z36 2010
    302.3—dc22   2010005534

FIRST EDITION

15 14 13 12 11 10   10 9 8 7 6 5 4 3 2 1

Cover art and design: Randi Hazan
Author photo: Parris Whittingham
Copyeditor: Elissa Rabellino
Production, interior design, and composition: Leigh McLellan Design

Contents

Preface   ix

1 The Power of Sharing   *1*

Welcome to the Future, or, The Birth of Sharing   *2*

Sharing for the Rest of Us   *4*

How the Magic Happens   *6*

Freedom of Information Act(ion)   *9*

How Connectors Feed the Magic of Sharing   *12*

Onward, Young Sharer   *14*

2 Are We There Yet?   *15*

Why the Aggregation of Influence Is a Bad Thing   *16*

A Brief State of the Internet Union   *17*

The Dangers of Replicating Bias and Exclusion
  Online   *21*

Won't Mobile Fix Everything?   *26*

Change, Not Band-Aids   *28*

3 We Are What You Share   *29*

Trading in Karma   *29*

On the Internet, Everybody Knows You're a Dog   *35*

Your Life Makes History   *39*

Diving In   *43*

How Sharing Inspires Social Change   *46*

Authenticity, the Great Equalizer   *50*

Know Your Network, Know Yourself   *51*

4 Trust Everyone   *55*

The Anatomy of Organic Authority   *56*

Institutional Authority on the Hot Seat   *57*

Size Doesn't Matter—Relationships Do   *59*

Avoiding the Newest Numbers Trap   *62*

An Abundance of Attention   *65*

Information Wildfires   *68*

I'm Not Dead Yet: Stopping Info Misflow   *69*

When Twittering Goes Awry   *71*

Lessons of Iran's Aftermath   *73*

Your Networks Save the Day   *75*

Your Network's Role in Building and
    Managing Your Authority—Sanely   *78*

Playing by New Rules   *80*

5 Sharing Is Daring *81*
• • • • • • • • • • • • • • •

Free-For-All Organizing, and the Secret
   Tyrants We All Are *81*

How to Be a Useful Agent of Change *87*

Lions and Tigers and Bears! Oh, My(Space)!
   The Fears People Have **89**

The Monsters Under the Bed *91*

The Benefits Far Outweigh the Hard Parts *100*

CONCLUSION What the Future Holds *103*
• • • • • • • • • • • • • • • • • • • • • • • • • •

RESOURCES
• • • • • • • • • •

Yeah, But… *107*

Tips for Individuals *115*

Tactics for Organizations *127*

Crowdfunding *Share This!* *143*

Notes & Treats *149*

Acknowledgments *163*

Index *167*

About the Author *173*

• • • • • • • • • • • • • • •

for my mom, Rachael

Preface

• • • • • • • •

HEY! YOU. Yes, you, right there. Did you know that posting what you had for breakfast, offering advice about parenting, and posting links to news stories you find interesting all have the potential to radically change the world?

No?

Then this book is for you.

Social networking is all the rage, and it's coming at us, a million miles an hour. We're surrounded by a flurry of new technology, and just when we begin to make sense of one tool, a new one arrives on the scene. (At the time of this writing, we are predominantly using what you out there in The Future may remember as Facebook, Twitter, LinkedIn, and MySpace.)

All this activity leaves us little time to contemplate any forest for all these trees, let alone think about the bigger picture of how this technology will change the future. But here's the secret: *How we share information, find community, and both connect and disconnect will give us unprecedented influence over our place in the world.* Social media technology holds some of the biggest potential for creating tectonic shifts in how we operate, and the overall open-ended promise of technology gives us a great shot at creating the systems for change. Technology isn't a magic bullet for solving the world's problems, but it's certainly a spark to the fastest fuse to explode our notions of power that the world has seen in a thousand years. In this book, I hope to show you how to light that fuse.

It hasn't been easy to thrive in our culture for the last hundred years or so. We've become ever more obsessed with consumption and power. Our corporate mass media and politicians have been treating us as faceless members of large demographics with open wallets, and less as individuals within communities, leading us down dark paths of apathy and isolation. We've had little room for recourse and little chance to connect to one another.

All of that's changing, and rapidly. People are using social technologies to find and connect. A study from the Pew Internet & American Life Project in November 2009 showed that people who have Internet access and/or a mobile phone were much more likely to have bigger, more diverse discussion networks, for example.[1] As I argue in this book, when we connect and share our lives with one another, both in the digital space and in the physical space, we create bonds of trust and empathy that lead us away from that apathy that's glazed over our eyeballs for at least a century. Our lives matter: What we believe and which truths we hold to be self-evident *matter*.

Along the way, I stress that technology is a tool, a means—never the end. It's important to remember that these tools are never completely neutral (because of the biases tech innovators can bring to the table), and that, to achieve its full potential, sharing in social networks requires complementary forms of organizing, activism, electoral work, and policy advocacy.

Your presence is required in this work: We need you in the online social space. Desperately. We have a tremendous opportunity to bring in voices previously marginalized or dismissed when it comes to shaping public conversations. But change won't happen on its own—it requires you to show up, and to participate.

If you choose to sit this one out, though, your void causes a ripple effect. First, your own reputation, something that's increasingly important as recommendation and referral become cornerstones of how we operate, will suffer because you're not there building and managing it. Then, because you're not contributing to the larger, very public conversations about what's happening in the world and how problems should be solved, others will define and direct the conversation without the benefit of your experiences and knowledge. Y'know, like what's been going on for the last few thousand years.

Here's the thing: I truly believe that through social networking, we can influence the way these conversations affect how change happens. As more conversations are taking place in public, we can represent ourselves. We can break stereotypes. We can transform our new connections into social change.

I hereby offer you an ambassadorship to a more democratic future. Do you choose to accept this mission?

Who This Book Is For
• • • • • • • • • • • • • • • •

Let's start out with some basic assumptions about who you are and why social media matters to you. Then, if you're reading this in the bookstore and wondering whether it is *really* the book for you, you'll know. (And likely, you'll buy it. Won't you? It's so nice and slim and trim, so easy to carry around or take on vacation with you. It's practically *bought itself*.)

People have wildly varied experiences and all kinds of questions about technology, and I'm going to make a few assumptions right at the outset. I'm going to assume, for the purpose of this introduction, that many of you are comfortable with computers and the Internet in general. You have an e-mail account or two.

You've shopped online, and you've got Google nailed. You've heard of social networks, "Web 2.0," and social media, and might belong to a few services. If you do, you use them, but you're not obsessive (like *some* people). You might have a friend or daughter (hi, Mom!) writing a book about the power of social media to induce systemic cultural and political change, but that's a little less likely. Hey, who knows? You're reading this book to figure out What It All Means.[2]

Which brings me to my other crew: There's a group of you out there who are interested in social change and activism. You've been bonked over the head with the idea that social technology can help you to achieve your goals. You've read some articles about how to do fund-raising online or have heard that organizations are having success getting new people interested in their work through social media. In short, you're trying to make sense of this intersection of social justice and technology before it slips through your fingers and evolves into something else, and you don't feel like you've had the chance to grasp what's happening in the first place.

Why I Wrote This Book
• • • • • • • • • • • • • • • • •

Many forces—technological, social, economic, and political— have converged to a place where we can all dive in and make change happen. I decided to write this book to explain the shift that's under way and to show you how you're going to change the world. You, li'l ol' you right there.

I'm a social media strategist who provides planning, workshops, and training on social networking for organizations and people looking to change the world. I came into the world a geek—in 1982, when I was seven, instead of buying a video game console, my parents brought home a personal computer for my brother and me to mess around with. In my late teens,

I became politically conscious and realized that the world's problems weren't going to fix themselves. My inner activist kicked in. When the Internet invaded my life in 1994, I saw the huge potential ahead of us—*and* the huge amount of work.

By 2003, I'd quit my nine-to-five job in order to commit myself to technology and activism. I've worked with progressive media and advocacy organizations, helping them to get beyond preaching to audiences and instead to explore ways to connect to their communities. AlterNet.org, Jim Hightower's *Hightower Lowdown*, GRITtv with Laura Flanders, Feministing.com, the Women's Media Center, and the Media Consortium are among the many I've had the pleasure of working with. They've taught me that, while it's fun for tech folk like me to bat around ideas, there's still a lot of work to be done in developing technologies that enhance our work in social change, and a lot of work in connecting people to the right technologies to fit their missions. One size does not fit all, and there is no easy answer.

My approach to social media has been heavily influenced by my participation in and organizing of social justice and change projects without formal organizations running them. The Hurricane Information Center, started in 2008 by NPR's Andy Carvin, for example, was a collection of tools gathered and utilized by hundreds of *volunteers* helping hurricane victims prepare for, evacuate, and recover from devastating storms. Later that year, I also worked on the Twitter Vote Report project, in which a number of volunteers used Twitter, texting, mapping, and other technologies to enable voters to report problems at their polling places. Previously, my experiences in offline, ad-hoc organizing, particularly the arts-related projects my cohorts and I developed during the Republican National Convention in 2004, gave me a strategic education that could be applied to online projects. These experiences made it clear to me that the freely available nature of the tools reduces some of the complexity of organizing.

We no longer have to rely on the old ways of top-down, or even organization-based, grassroots organizing.

As a woman all too familiar with the "pale, male, and stale" phenomenon,[3] I also understand that diversity is key to bringing about tremendous social change using social technology. And I believe it's critical to acknowledge the privilege one brings to the table: The social system we live in automatically gives people benefits based on the color of their skin, the money they have, their gender, their sexuality, their access to technology, and more. I recognize that my privilege influences the work I do, and if I lose sight of that fact, I expect to be reminded and held responsible.

What This Book Isn't

To be clear about what we're going to get done, I should tell you right off the bat that this isn't the End-All-Be-All Activist's Guide to Fixing Everything with Social Networking. (That's why we didn't call it that, for starters.) There are plenty of books and websites that will tell you how to raise money, how to get people to sign petitions, how to get people to call their senators, all with social networking. We'll go over some thoughtful tactics toward the end of the book, but the thrust is going to be on the individual's role in transforming our culture and thus our world to be more livable for everyone. We won't get into the nitty-gritty of each tool that's out there, and we won't be dissecting case study after case study. We also won't be addressing the future of traditional media in this book. While we touch on the role that traditional media plays in advancing social change through telling stories, we won't be able to tackle the hard topics of what the future of journalism holds. I'll be concentrating mostly on web-based technologies, only discussing others—mobile/SMS, e-mail, and so on—where overlap occurs. There are simply too many technologies, all changing almost daily, to cover in a static book. And even though I focus on the power of social technologies, don't forget: That's all relative to what else is happening in the world, and we still need loads of other kinds of organizing and activism to complement what we share.

What's Ahead
• • • • • • • • • •

This book is designed to walk you through the ins and outs—the opportunities and potential pitfalls—of the social networking landscape, viewed through the lens of social change. I've also created the illustrations and graphics to help you visualize new concepts. In chapter 1, "The Power of Sharing," we'll discuss how the tools help us to transcend the traditional ways of communicating that too often restrict our ability to effect change. But as much as many of us would like to believe the Internet is a promised land of meritocracy, it isn't. Chapter 2, "Are We There Yet?" shows how we reproduce social structures online that marginalize voices and prevent meaningful advancement.

In chapter 3, "We Are What You Share," we'll learn that there's more to social networks than just posting minutiae: Through sharing with others, we ultimately build the trust and empathy that are the building blocks of any movement for change. Your participation is critical. Chapter 4, "Trust Everyone," argues that we can subvert traditional power structures through choosing who is important, relevant, and interesting—and we do this by deciding to whom we assign authority. But we need to guard against the temptation to let shiny new things get the best (or worst, as it were) of us.

Discomfort, fears, and hesitations sometimes keep us out of conversations we need to be joining; chapter 5, "Sharing Is Daring," shows us how to overcome them. And in the Conclusion, we'll get a glimpse of where we're headed at this juncture of social change and technology.

Finally, the "Resources" section offers a collection of tips and tools designed to help you be your own best advocate for making change though social media. "Yeah, But . . ." provides responses to the most common objections to social media; it's the ammunition you need to build your confidence and win that argument around the water cooler. In "Tips for Individuals," you'll find hands-on advice, from getting started to more advanced and nuanced guidance; "Tactics for Organizations" offers fundamentals that organizations need to keep in mind, as well as essential pieces for the tool kit. And in "Crowdfunding *Share This!*" I've included the tale of how this book got funded, as a case study in the power of social capital and community building.

And We're Off!

When I wrote in these pages that we're going to "change the world," I expressed my fundamental conviction that change starts with each one of us—the "Be the change you wish to see in the world" ethos from Gandhi. When we're connecting, sharing, and changing the understanding of the people around us, we are at the beginning of making the world a better place. Activism always starts with stories, and we each have a unique contribution to make to the Grand Permanent Record of Things. From there, sharing can lead to advocacy success, electoral wins, and policy changes. We'll talk about some strategies and tactics for that kind of change, but before we get there, we have to commit personally to uprooting our notions of how things work and to reaching out to those around us. The commitment to sharing our experiences with one another supports and strengthens our bonds, and *we* are our own best hope for changing the world.

I promise: We're about to have a really good time.

1 　 The Power of Sharing

SOMETHING FUNDAMENTAL about change has not changed at all: Stories still come first. Before any change happens, online or offline—before you get your phone banking, your petitions, your door knocking, your lobby days, your e-mail campaigns, your anything—change starts with stories. *Our* stories. Storytelling has been the most powerful building block for social change since the beginning of time—think about how long humans have been sitting around the campfire telling each other what's going on. Social networking gives us unprecedented power to share our stories with more people than we ever imagined.

What happens when you tell stories? Two magical things: You build trust with other people in your network, and from there you build empathy. Note that I'm not talking about sympathy. *Sym*pathy is when you feel badly for people who have had something bad happen to them. *Em*pathy is when you share the emotions that other people have and express. It's a powerful, deeply primal experience.

The trust we create on social networks fuels the empathetic response we have to one another, even if we don't know each other that well. All of us have stories, experiences, and opinions to share as foundations for the change we make in the world.

As we'll see, sharing subverts our traditional notions of power around information, and it offers a must-seize occasion for democratization.

Welcome to the Future, or, The Birth of Sharing

In order to understand why sharing offers such a radical opportunity to create a better world, it's helpful to understand the origins of the World Wide Web. That history shows, pointedly, how the web's origin is a story not just about whizbang technology; it's more fundamentally about great human drive—the primal need to interact with people who have similar experiences, values, and goals.

Although the Internet has been around for 40 years,[1] it was largely the provenance of military researchers and academics until some Very Important Things happened. In early 1992, there were "26 reasonably reliable"[2] servers connected to one another, forming the World Wide Web. By late 1993, that number had grown to more than 200,[3] and a trifecta of events occurred within a few months of each other to send the WWW hurtling toward the mainstream:

- A lot of users had been using something called Gopher, developed by the University of Minnesota, to share documents. The university made a very silly judgment call: It decided to charge organizations that wanted to use this technology on their servers.[4] That decision caused server administrators to explore other free options; the World Wide Web, just gaining traction, was quite attractive.

- Then CERN,[5] the organization that was "in charge" of the technology behind the WWW, decided that it *wouldn't* charge for licensing the tech and that it would make the code readily available to anyone who was interested.

- Finally, Marc Andreessen, who had left NCSA[6] in '93 to start a company focused on web software, publicly released the first version of Mosaic after earlier versions had gained popularity among academics.[7] It was one of the first graphical web browsers accessible for everyday folks to use, and one of the first to display images "inline," or within the web page. Inline images were a huge leap! Mosaic and the company that Andreessen founded eventually became Netscape.

Voilà, the rush to the WWW was born. But it was very different from what it looks like now. If we wanted to publish something online—think of the web then as being almost like a library with an infinite amount of space and few books in it—here are the hurdles we might have encountered. First, we'd have to get access to a server that was connected to the web. Access was fairly limited, as most of the web was being used for academic purposes, and online services such as Prodigy, AOL, and CompuServe wanted customers to stay within the neat walled garden of content they provided. Even the WELL,[8] a nerd-famous online community started in 1985 in San Francisco, while having a more open policy for getting on board with the web, had its own members-only, non-web content (which it continued to maintain for a number of years).

Once we had server access, we (or someone we knew) had to know Hyper Text Markup Language (HTML), the language that's used to present documents on the web. It was pretty simple compared with actual programming languages, but it was created by geeks for geeks. Anyone could learn HTML, but a certain bent toward the nerdy was required to get into it.

Once we finished putting those documents in HTML, we'd have to transfer them to the web server so that they could be "served," or viewed by others. Each one would have its own unique URL that we could then share with our friends. Sharing the documents could be tricky. Few people had e-mail, and probably fewer had Internet access that would allow them to work with documents online. The few who did have access and e-mail (again, mostly people at universities or in certain workplaces) could go to the links and read the documents. To share feedback, they'd have to send private messages to the author of the document, or if they belonged to some sort of group messaging service, such as a listserv, they could offer comments to the group. Everything operated within *closed systems*, which meant that the conversation was contained within its own sphere, with little to no extension into public conversations.

Sharing for the Rest of Us

Cowboy capitalism took over the initial period of the web's mainstream explosion, but it wasn't long before the human drive to connect and share rose out of the ashes of the dot-com boom/bust.

Despite the fact that technological hurdles prevented everyday people from being able to publish and participate on the web early on, market forces allowed people with capital and resources to jump right in. If you personally didn't have the skills to create web pages and maintain a server, or you didn't belong to those networks that had access to the Internet, you could simply purchase a server, hire a few nerds, and head on down the merry way toward the Wild West of the Internet.

The people who were willing, in the early days, to risk spending that kind of money were investors who either saw the light or knew they could make their money back. Soon, those folks with the cash began driving the development of services available on the web, in an effort to maximize the return on their investment. The web, during the ramp-up of what became known as the "dot-com boom," became less about people sharing information with one another (how can you make money on *that*?) and more about creating ways for people to buy and sell products to each other.

The web became a market paradise, a capitalist's *dream*. While there were still plenty of people working on more social applications—forums come to mind—the cultural focus, as is wont to happen, shifted toward commercialism. It took less money and less know-how to sell on the web than it did to set up a brick-and-mortar business, but it certainly took *some*. Which was way more than most had.

Lo and behold, in 2000, bubbles burst, and the dot-com boom ended a few years into its silliness. Note that the Internet didn't pack itself up and wander off; innovation and a dedication to refining applications continued. What emerged out of those ashes was, in many ways, a return to the original ethos of the web: making it easy for people to share information.

One of the more well-known products/services to come out of this drive was blog software. In 1999 and 2000, some technologically inclined people started to realize that manually updating their web pages was kind of a drag, and developers (like proto-blogger Dave Winer, Evan Williams of Blogger and the guys behind LiveJournal) started producing software that would simplify the process. *Weblog* first came into use in 1997; its shortened version, *blog,* was meant to be a joke, but Williams popularized the term with his Blogger software.[9] Soon enough, people gained the ability to share and publish their experiences and opinions without a lot of technical know-how.

Progressive activists started using early web technologies to share stories not being covered in mainstream, traditional media. In response to the desire to offer alternative news reportage about the World Trade Organization protests in Seattle in 1999, a group of media activists founded the first Independent Media

Center (IMC).[10] Anyone in the IMC model could publish and share news stories; the idea caught on in other cities worldwide following the protests, and a large decentralized network of IMCs formed in the following years.

Also in the late 1990s, basic social networks were launched. One of the most prominent was Classmates.com (which is still around), while one of my favorites, SixDegrees.com,[11] went defunct in the bubble. SixDegrees was particularly revolutionary because it allowed you to look for other members and see how you were connected to them—very Kevin Bacon.[12] Many websites started including social networking features, such as the ability to add friends, and to share links and content with them.

By the early 2000s, sites whose main function was social networking started to spring up—who here remembers Friendster? MySpace, Black Planet, MiGente, hi5, Xanga, Facebook, and Ning all followed shortly thereafter, not to mention more informal social networks that were created around content-sharing sites like YouTube (video sharing), Flickr (picture sharing), and Delicious (bookmark sharing). Mobile technologies had also matured to a point where SMS texting became fairly common in many demographics, as well as did surfing the web via cell phones. When Twitter took the tech elite by storm at the SXSW Interactive conference in 2007, social networks were granted staying power. The seeds of change had been firmly planted into the culture.

How the Magic Happens

The difference between old ways of communicating and what's happening on the Internet now is the *digitization* of our relationships and networks. Social networks are not a new phenomenon—people have belonged to numerous networks since the beginning of humanity. Think of your own social spheres, which may include work friends, family members, and neighbors. Now picture them not just as isolated from one another in our minds, but also as overlapping at some points, and connected in public through you. We're sharing information about ourselves and our networks online, which leads to more connections with other people and other networks. The mapping of those connections via online social network tools—in essence, creating large information pipes that didn't previously exist—puts communication methods like word-of-mouth on steroids *and* speed.

The traditional media (cable news channels, newspapers and magazines, etc.) have a love-hate relationship with social technology—and with good reason. This technology is revolutionizing how we send and receive information. It's not just that our current media structures are threatened (they are); it's also that an entire shift is happening, both in how we obtain information and in what we do with that information once we've processed it.

For starters, we're not just consuming information; we're *sharing* it, immediately and constantly. When we read a news story online, there's usually a tool on the page that encourages us to "e-mail this to a friend" or post it to one of dozens of social networks. When we watch a funny video, we embed it on our own site or link to it so that others will watch. When something happens that makes us go "Wow!" we want to tell everyone we know.

And we can. But our sharing power reaches beyond our own personal relationships to the relationships and networks of our friends, and their friends', and so on.

Picture billions of soap bubbles in a sink. Each bubble represents a different person, and the bubble size reflects that person's sphere of influence. Where bubbles connect and intersect represents our relationships with people around us.

We've always belonged to multiple spheres, but in the offline world, the piece that was missing was clear documentation

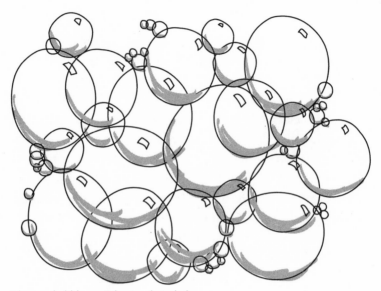

Like soap bubbles, social networks include connected elements of varying size of influence.

or mapping of those relationships. We could exchange information about ourselves, but physical limitations and social expectations prevented us from widespread information sharing. You wouldn't, say, set up a conference call with a bunch of people you knew casually to talk about your family vacation—it would have been expensive and culturally weird.

Now, using a variety of tools—e-mail, social networks like Facebook and MySpace, and microblogging services like Twitter—we have the ability to create *maps* of our relationships. I don't mean maps in the pictorial sense, like a giant family tree. I mean maps in the pathway sense. We are able to create and use direct pathways to engage in immediate, many-to-many conversations with people in our social networks by sharing our experiences with one another.

Those pathways create ways for us to take advantage of our relationships in revolutionary ways, particularly when we share information with each other, rather than simply receiving information passively from sources outside of our personal relationships.

Freedom of Information Act(ion)
••••••••••••••••••••••••••

Information has been released from hierarchical constraints, to some degree.

The old way of doing things involved a fairly complex hierarchy, one that many of you are probably (painfully) familiar with. We can simplify that hierarchy into a pyramid shape for the purposes of this discussion:

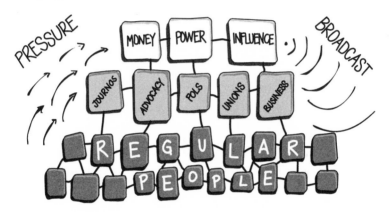

At the bottom of the food chain, there are the everyday people. You and me. We've all got connections and relationships, but to get anything significant done in the world, it's helpful to be connected to people higher up in the hierarchy. Of course, very few people are.

In the middle is a conglomeration of folks with more influence and power—journalists, midlevel politicians, owners of sizable businesses, as well as advocacy organizations and some labor unions. In the media subset, journalists are pressured and pitched by folks both above and below, and the stories that result (or don't) are not always fair or comprehensive.

Everyday folks can organize and push up onto bigger levels to get their stories told. Working on their own (less effective) or in groups (the more the merrier), people can petition, write letters to the editor, make calls, and use online tools to make their voices heard. It's a constant struggle, this pushing up, and invariably some voices don't make the cut.

In the upper echelons, you'll find the bigger decision makers and power brokers. High-level politicians, media moguls—pretty much anyone who can issue any kind of mandate. They're giving directives to the folks in the middle about what the folks at the bottom want to hear. It's like a giant pyramid with information traveling upwards, slowing to a trickle as it gets to the top. Then, because it's mostly a broadcast medium, the information is released from the top and heads downward—a constant, fast-moving flood.

Of course, information is also shared laterally—passed via word of mouth within and sometimes between levels. But for the most part, our mass communications have operated for centuries within a pretty rigid pyramid structure.

While the pyramid game of top-down-bottom-up may still be desirable at times, it's now no longer as necessary to play. To return to the soap bubble metaphor, effective communication is much more about sharing within networks and connecting to new folks who share your interests. Social media tools make it wonderfully easy to do just that.

Already we've seen cases in which everyday people have used the relationships they've fostered on social networks to do good. In the summer of 2009, for example, the Palm Beach County School District announced a controversial new academic program that centralized authority over teaching programs and increased the emphasis on standardized tests.[13] Parents throughout the school system were upset with the changes. Soon after the announcement, a substitute teacher and parent named Lisa

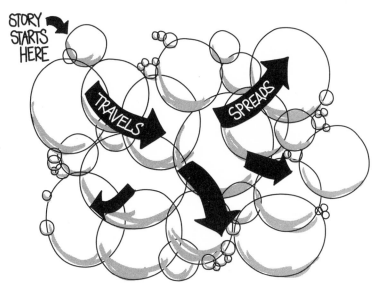

STORY STARTS HERE

TRAVELS

SPREADS

How stories travel on social networks.

Goldman started a Facebook page called "Testing Is Not Teaching!"[14] where people in the community could come together and share information and action ideas.

After a critical school board meeting, the group ballooned to more than a thousand members, and after just five weeks in existence it had expanded to more than six thousand members. Several months into the fight, school administrators agreed to meet with members of the group, and in October 2009, the superintendent of the school system agreed to let individual principals of schools decide which parts of the plan they would adopt. Goldman and a comanager continue to press on for the reversal of the program.[15]

Goldman and her group didn't have to rely solely on traditional modes of getting the word out about their issue or spend as much time offline organizing their fellow parents as they would have in the past. They were able to tap into existing relationships and social networks (Goldman cites the strength of the relationships between mothers in the community in particular) quickly and effectively through Facebook.

Advocacy and messaging in the social networking sphere is not so much about broadcasting to a billion people with the hope that a few care about the information they're receiving, as it is about targeting a smaller, more invested number of individuals and letting them share the information they're concerned about with their own networks.

How Connectors Feed the Magic of Sharing
• •

Some people play another important, very specialized role in passing on stories through social networks. These people have large spheres of influence that are based on their connections to many different groups. Malcolm Gladwell spends a great deal of time talking about these folks in his book *The Tipping Point.* These are his "Connectors":

> Sprinkled among every walk of life . . . are a handful of people with a truly extraordinary knack of making friends and acquaintances. . . .
>
> They are people whom all of us can reach in only a few steps because, for one reason or another, they occupy many different worlds and subcultures and niches.[16]

Connectors create two main types of relationships that play a large role in social media. First, there are the obvious *strong ties*—close friendships, business relationships, romances, family.[17] They are the people with whom we come into contact regularly, and we have a deep, core understanding of one another.

Then there are what sociologists refer to as *weak ties*. Weak ties can be people with whom we have random, light, infrequent interactions. Maybe you sat next to someone at a conference and exchanged contact info, and you only run into each another at that kind of event.

Weak ties can also represent the idea that we *might* know or be interested in each other simply based on the number of people we have in common. If I have 20 friends on Facebook, and I see that 10 of them are friends with you, then there is a chance that we share some commonality.

Making and maintaining weak ties used to require a special sort of person—someone whom Gladwell describes as having "some combination of curiosity, self-confidence, sociability, and energy." Maintaining weak ties, before the explosion of social technologies, took a lot of work.

Because social technologies now make it easier to stay both loosely *and* tightly connected to one another, it's more convenient than ever for all of us to maintain weak ties. But in many ways, Connectors play an even larger role than ever because of the multiple worlds they move within. It's no longer as important to be at the top of some social pecking order to have a major impact on how far we spread information.

In the case of "Testing Is Not Teaching!" let's say that people are blogging and commenting on social networks about the academic program, coming at it from different angles. There's the educational value angle of the story, there are class and race implications of standardized testing, and there are local-politics angles that are being discussed. If enough people are talking about it, a Connector is going to notice the chatter across different spheres, and that person will likely post it to their social networks, thus spreading the story out even farther.

When these Connector folks get involved, mainstream media, politicians, and others at the top of the old hierarchy start to take notice. That hierarchy (unfortunately) isn't completely going away anytime soon, so getting people with influence on board might still be important. But the distribution of information doesn't have to start with those "in charge."[18]

Onward, Young Sharer
••••••••••••••••••

We're living through the emergence of a complementary form of information distribution through social technology tools, one that has the potential to shift and, in many cases, dissolve the information hierarchies that have existed for thousands of years. The web is just now starting to realize some of its disruptive potential, and the digitization of our social networks give us a great opportunity to shift power dynamics away from those hierarchical constraints.

We each have a significant contribution to make to that shift, and sharing our stories with one another on the grand scale that social networks provide is the place to start. The events, opinions, and experiences we choose to share don't just matter on a hyper-local level (within the tighter parts of our social networks); they also have ripple effects through others' networks as they spread. You may remember, for example, an upstart long-shot presidential candidate with a funny name from 2008, who harnessed the energy for change found in social networks—and won. World-changing ideas start with a few individuals sharing with and relating to one another.

But before we can say that it's all smooth sailing in the world of social networking, it's important to identify the structural and cultural biases that keep everyone from participating. Without everyone's voices being heard, our next great leap toward progress is in danger.

2   Are We There Yet?

NO DOUBT ABOUT IT: Social networks have landed in our culture, and they're planning to stay a while.

During late 2008 and early 2009, Facebook doubled in size, growing from 100 million registered users to 200 million in eight months,[1] and then added another 150 million users by early 2010.[2] Twitter's popularity skyrocketed during most of 2009, jumping from 4.5 million visitors to more than 20 million.[3]

And yet, for all those impressive numbers, and for all the horn-tootin' that happens about the disruptive and democratizing potential of the Internet, we're still seeing the Big Important Conversations being dominated by the same old, same old.[4] Despite the fact that women, for example, make up over half of the active users on most social networking sites,[5] we still usually see men served up as the expert voices on social networks, on blogs, and in mainstream media. Or, even though African-Americans who are online are more likely to be users of Twitter than white people who are online,[6] white people are given the role of experts for speaking at conferences, on top 10 lists, and more. In 2009, for example, Europe's top web conference, LeWeb, had mind-bogglingly few speakers who were women (just 5%) or people of color (under 10%).[7] We're asked to listen to the same voices that got us to where we are today, socially and culturally; and often when there's homogeneity in the experts' background, there's also a lack of ideological diversity. Structural, societal forces that keep diverse voices separate from one another are pressing down on us as participants and reinforcing existing hierarchies. If the Internet is so revolutionary, why are we still stuck with more of the same?

Why the Aggregation of Influence Is a Bad Thing

Money, influence, and access congregate around those who do the talking. The same folks get the attention—and thus the resources—to put forth ideas and issues. Clay Shirky, author and faculty member at the Interactive Telecommunications Program at New York University, examined what's known as "the power law" back in 2003.[8] According to the power law, the more well-known something becomes, the more exponentially its popularity increases. For example, you don't get twice as popular when two people like you; you actually get at least four times more popular, thanks to those two people's combined influence.

Looking at the number of incoming links to a variety of blogs (433 in total), Shirky found that just two blogs held a full 5% of all inbound links. And blogs aren't the only place online where he found power law distributions. Therefore, the Internet is serving to replicate age-old patterns of influence and power.

Creating a just society is sort of like the evolution of a species. If you have a bunch of the same DNA mixing together, the species mutates poorly and eventually dies off. But bring in variety—new strains of DNA—and you create a stronger species. It's no different in idea generation. You get a bunch of the same people talking to each other and making the rules for a few millennia, and eventually you're going to end up with a lack of meaningful advancement.

It's time to bring fresh life into the conversations that we're having about social change, and social networks are our strongest bets for doing so. A November 2009 Pew Internet & American Life study showed, for example, that people who use a social networking service have networks that are about 20% more diverse than people who don't use the Internet at all.[9] By being connected to different types of people with whom we share our stories, we're setting the stage for a fundamental shift in how we make change.

I think we can change the traditional power dynamics. In fact, I think *you will* change the traditional power dynamics.

A tremendous amount of *potential* for Internet culture exists, but it's just now being realized. I hear what you're saying: "I remember 1995, too! That's when everyone said the Internet was this big democracy, and the whole 'No one knows you're a dog online' stuff. But that didn't happen, did it?"

No, not yet.

As Karen Carpenter once sang, "We've only just begun."

A Brief State of the Internet Union

Before we tackle the "how" end of the question, let's have a look at the cultural and ideological ecosphere known as the Internet as it stands now:

- Although broadband access at home is growing every year, minorities still lag behind. For example, while 63% of all American homes now have broadband Internet service, only 46% of African-American homes do.[10]

- Half of the 20% of Americans who have dial-up connections or don't go on the Internet at all say that it's not relevant to their lives.[11]

MAKING LESS THAN $40,000
WHO TOOK ACTION ONLINE

MAKING $100,000 OR MORE
WHO TOOK ACTION ONLINE

- Only 18% to 20% of adults making less than $40,000 a year took some kind of political action online between August 2007 and August 2008, compared with 45% of people making $100,000 a year.[12]

- Of young adults who are online and actively participating in creating content, 64% of men have shared content that they created online, while only 50% of women have.[13]

- Wikipedia says its contributors—that is, people who are editing our history—are "more than 80 percent male, more than 65 percent single, more than 85 percent without children, around 70 percent under the age of 30."[14]

Does diversity even matter when it comes to technology and who's active online? We've come this far and gotten some pretty cool stuff out of the deal, so do we need to be all that concerned?

Well, *yes*. The ideas that we come up with through sharing and connecting on social networks—especially those that tackle the tough issues of social change—fundamentally require participation from lots of people with different experiences and identities in order to succeed. We're not talking about making sure you have a person of color in your friends list, or even that your organization's constituency has the demographically sound representative number of women. Diversity in the social network sphere is critical for generating fresh perspectives on old problems, to help us avoid replicating on the Internet what we've done for hundreds of years—marginalizing or otherwise ignoring voices that can share ideas for systemic change.

In the old way, gatekeepers had the most influence on things like news and policy. Gatekeepers have traditionally been made up of classes of people[15] who didn't typically question the social, economic, or political status quo.[16] It's a status quo that's brought us an unemployment rate that is always much higher for people of color than for white people (and that gap is widening),[17] 7,783 reported incidents of hate crimes in the United States in 2008,[18] the rates of violence against women skyrocketing in recent years,[19] the fact that LGBT youth are four times more likely to attempt suicide than straight youth (not to mention that 30% to 50% of all transgender people have attempted suicide),[20] and the largest gap between rich and poor since the Great Depression.[21] Up till now, we've clearly been living out a definition of insanity often attributed to either Einstein or Ben Franklin: doing the same things over and over and expecting different results. Remember that DNA theory I mentioned in the last section? A bunch of the same material has been mixing around the save-the-world gene pool, and the possibilities for innovation are exhausted. In 2007, for example, the website kottke.org surveyed the most prominent tech conferences in 2006 and 2007 in search of female speakers.[22] The numbers were dismal: The highest percentage, outside of a tech conference specifically for women, was 30%, and most hovered in the 10% to 15% range. We've got to infuse new ideas into the mix.

When addressing inequality, too often we look at, and for, the voices of authorized experts to establish what needs to be done. More often than not, those experts come out of a tiny demographic not representative of who is affected most by the injustices we're working on. Technology-related policy wonks and thought leaders are especially white and male, even though women and people of color make up large swaths (even majorities) of technology users in many cases, and thus are creating policy and environments with only their worldview, based on only their experiences.

"Leave it to the experts" may work in a number of environments, especially those constrained to traditional top-down hierarchal structures, but the Internet's open platform makes such traditional constraints outmoded and even damaging. Joshua Breitbart, policy director for the People's Production House, in a talk about the importance of featuring diverse perspectives when addressing Internet access inequality, stated, "We knew from our allies that policy should be driven by the people most affected by it. So we figured, if you want to make the Internet work for more people, you don't leave the policy decisions to the people for whom it already works perfectly."[23]

We need to use a multivectored approach to address digital inequality. Installing high-speed cables to every home won't magically erase the divisions—often by class and race—in how people are able to benefit from using the Internet. Unfortunately, many do not understand the kind of nuanced conversations that are necessary. "One size just does not fit all," says Shireen Mitchell, a social media consultant specializing in issues with women of color online. "We just don't seem to understand that yet. The problems of exclusion still run deep, and many people do not see them."[24] Addressing digital inequality must take into account larger systemic and cultural divides that both create the inequality and reinforce it.

We desperately need the perspectives of all different kinds of people when we're addressing how technology will assist us in changing the world. We can't grow as a society if we're listening to, critiquing, and circling around the same voices, from the same background.

The Dangers of Replicating Bias and Exclusion Online

We're living like fish in water on the Internet right now: We don't know, or we're not willing to recognize, that we're soaking in the same social structures we've been living with for hundreds, maybe thousands, of years. We're porting our understanding of the offline world—with all our prejudices, biases, and hierarchies—onto the blank canvas of the Internet. But all we can see is the blank canvas; we remain convinced that the Internet is a pure meritocracy and that if you just work hard enough, you'll succeed at whatever it is that you're trying to do. We've got to interrupt this pattern now, with conscious effort and action.

Before we can get very far into examining social networking's potential to disrupt and dismantle un- and antidemocratic power structures, we should take a step back and look at who's on the Internet and what they're able to do. "Multiple digital divides" exist;[25] the one most folks look at first is who has Internet access at home. According to Pew Internet Research, broadband access at home is more popular than ever: In 2009, 63% of adults had a high-speed Internet connection at home, up from 55% in 2008.[26] Overall, there was particularly strong growth in recent years—even during a recession—for lower-income households: "Respondents reporting that they live in homes with annual household incomes below $30,000 experienced a 34% growth in home broadband adoption from 2008 to 2009."

Good news, right?

Well, yes, but there's also some bad news. As mentioned previously, African-Americans still reported the smallest amount of growth in the trend toward high-speed home connections, with only 46% saying they had broadband at home.

On top of looking at the pure numbers, we also tend to take on a blunt-force-object view when it comes to Internet access and factors like economic status and education. We assume that if people just get "onto the web," our problems of joblessness and lack of education will be solved. Unfortunately, such a one-dimensional view is not true, nor is it helpful for problem solving. As Breitbart notes: "From reading some reports, you might forget that poverty preceded the Internet. You might think that getting poor people online would magically make them wealthy."[27] Addressing the problems of Internet access and its relationship to societal and structural challenges requires us to understand their interdependent relationship.

Even if we were able to ensure universal access to the Internet, however, it wouldn't be enough to create a world that works for all. Users also need the appropriate skill sets to get the most out of the Internet. Access and expertise are inextricably intertwined. In the last 30 years, we've begun to think about media literacy (teaching skills for analyzing and thoughtfully processing messages we receive in media), but we need to add Internet-related processing skills to the mix. Youth of color particularly are being left out of the digital literacy conversation, compared with their white counterparts, notes Brian Smith, founder of What's Left Out.[28] "The effects of this can be seen every day," he writes. "Youth of color are using IT without adequate consideration or accurate knowledge of the consequences. I consider this lack of critical thinking a major contributor to the social issues plaguing communities of color." Without providing the new media literacy skills that come with the technology territory, we are leaving youth in the lurch for both their current social and learning needs, and their professional futures.

Unequal access to technology also severely limits the ability of users to develop skills over time. If your general status in life means that you can give your child a laptop to use any time that's convenient, your child will develop tech skills more intensely than a child who has to go to a library, where the time, physical space, and even content available are limited. Social technology researcher Estzer Hargittai describes a number of factors that complicate a technology user's skill development:

> Growing up in a household that has the latest gadgets and digital media resources will make a difference when a student encounters these tools in the classroom. Having siblings who can navigate the technologies will help in the transfer of relevant know-how. Living in neighborhoods where many in one's proximity are also discovering the latest information communication technology (ICT) options will allow for more opportunities to develop savvy in the domain of digital media than a situation in which one is isolated without access to relevant technologies and knowledgeable networks. . . . Overall, it is important to recognize that ICT do not nullify the effects of other variables on one's life chances. People's ICT uses happen in the context of their lives, influenced by their socioeconomic status and social surroundings.[29]

So, beyond providing access, we must take on the challenge of figuring out how to ensure that those online, with all of the different social and class elements involved, are developing sophisticated skills for getting the most out of the Internet. (And to those doing this work: Note that it's not just a matter of making sure the have-nots can do what the haves do; Breitbart points out, "[It] means, instead of trying to get people to use the Internet the way that we use it currently, we should be trying to adapt the Internet to work for more people."[30])

It's just as important for us to look at what people who are on board with social media are doing once they get there. Just as we do offline, people congregate at different services and networks online, and the reasons often have to do with identity. At the Personal Democracy Forum conference in 2009, noted technology researcher danah boyd gave a keynote talk to a largely white, middle- and upper-class audience on the realities of social stratification—the organizing of groups of people into hierarchies, often according to social and economic indicators—that occurs in social networks, and asked those in organizing and campaign jobs to recognize, account for, and make strategies that offset their biases. From her talk:

1. Social stratification is pervasive in American society (and around the globe). Social media does not magically eradicate inequality. Rather, it mirrors what is happening in everyday life and makes social divisions visible. . . .

2. There is no universal public online. . . . The digital publics that unfold highlight and reinforce structural divisions.

3. If you are trying to connect with the public, where you go online matters. . . . The key to developing a social media strategy is to understand who you're reaching and who you're not and make certain that your perspective is accounting for said choices. Understand your biases and work to counter them.

4. The Internet has enabled many new voices to enter the political fray, but not everyone is sitting at the table. There's a terrible tendency in this country, and especially among politically minded folks, to interpret an advancement as a solution. . . . The worst thing we can do is to walk away and congratulate ourselves for all of the good

things that have happened. Such attitudes create new breeding grounds for increased stratification.[31]

When we continue pretending that the Internet is a social utopia, we do a great disservice not just to each other, but also to younger generations and their understanding of how social networks function. Without the critical piece of tech literacy, they too are bound to repeat our cultural mistakes. In a 2006–2007 study, boyd found that teen users on social networks were not just seeking out those like themselves; they were also displaying typical class and racial tension toward users who didn't congregate where they did, who weren't like them. "What happened," she writes, "was modern day 'white flight.' Whites were more likely to leave or choose Facebook. The educated were more likely to leave or choose Facebook. . . . Those who deserted MySpace did so by 'choice' but their decision to do so was wrapped up in their connections to others."[32] This is not a legacy we want to leave, when there is so much more potential for fundamental change.

Looking through the gender lens, we also see signs of division and stratification. A 2008 study by RapLeaf, a researcher of social media trends, confirms that women make up just over half of all those participating in social networking activities,[33] but we see from other sources that old boys' networks are still being reinforced. In May 2009, for example, a *Harvard Business Review* study found that men are twice as likely to follow men instead of women on Twitter.[34] It's not just the numbers that matter (we'll talk more about that in chapter 4), it's the experience and perspective that are being shared. We can't get a clear picture of what life is really like in the world if we're all just talking to people like us.

In addition, women are more likely to use social networking to deepen their existing relationships (what's called *bonding* capital in social capital terms) rather than making loose, acquaintance-like new connections (known as *bridging* capital).[35] The focus on "deep" versus "many" connections can leave women out of the professional networking game in a big way, a dangerous proposition as our culture becomes increasingly reliant on relationships and connections.

It's time for us to commit to serious change. Remember, technology won't solve our problems. *We* will solve our problems, and in many cases technology will help us. We can't expect the latest and greatest gadgets and services to do the dirty work for us.

Won't Mobile Fix Everything?

Mobile devices are often touted as the way to overcome the digital access divides. Indeed, research has shown that mobile has very high penetration rates among groups of people that traditionally have been left out of the digital conversation. Especially in the United States, young Latinos have the highest rates of usage compared with any other demographic, for example.[36] Mobile technologies do present extraordinary *potential* tools for advancing fundamental change, but, I would argue, they are not the magic bullet that's going to solve our structural, societal woes.

When implemented effectively as part of an overall campaign strategy, mobile devices can do wonders for community organizing. In spring 2006, the immigration rallies and marches that drew millions into the streets across the United States used a blend of old-school community organizing, outreach on social networks, and what MobileActive.org cofounder Katrin Verclas calls "last-mile organizing"—reaching out to people where they are, using tech that's familiar to them—to achieve such numbers.[37] Teenagers walked out of schools as a result of organizers' using MySpace and text messaging to relay updated information as situations changed.[38] Mobile technologies can bridge gaps in organizing efforts with speed and efficiency.

Looking at social networks' relationship to cell phones, the numbers are surprising and enlightening. A good chunk of Twitter's usage comes from mobile devices, and Facebook reported that as of January 2010, it had more than 65 million engaged mobile users. In a blog post at iMedia Connection, James Briggs, CEO and founder of Briabe Media, points out three major areas for growth in this relationship:

- Social networks and mobile devices will continue to feed one another.

- More robust mobile social networks—for example, those that show location information—will become increasingly in demand.

- Mobile social network users are more active on the networks than their desktop counterparts.[39]

The way that mobile networks are set up, however, makes it difficult to engage users directly. For one thing, cell phone companies pretty much determine the policies of what's going to be distributed via their network and what isn't. That closed system differs from an *open* system like the Internet, which is ignorant of content (meaning it breaks everything down into bits and bytes and passes it along without knowing if it's an activist message or a sale ad for Penney's). For example, you know those short codes that you can send a text message to? Each cell phone company has to approve both the short code itself and the content it's going to be used for, making it more than challenging to turn good content into text-messaging-based campaigns and services.

The approval/rejection process is novel to cell phone networks and completely antithetical to how the web operates —where no permissions are needed to establish any kind of presence whatsoever. As Katrin Verclas told me, "It's not like on the web, where you buy a URL and that's that—your URL works on every Internet service provider." With cell phone companies, each one has to approve what you're doing.

Additionally, while mobile markets tend to reach more low-income folk, those people are actually paying more—largely through the use of prepaid services—per message and for usage than people on contract plans.

What does all this mean for diversity and access? Verclas suggests that any organization looking to get into mobile outreach go in with eyes wide open, as well as be ready to provide content that's going to be technologically and otherwise *relevant* to mobile users. Social change advocates will have to recognize the differing needs that people with mobile devices have, and create appropriate campaigns and content to inform and engage effectively.

Change, Not Band-Aids
••••••••••••••••••

As we've seen, these structural obstacles are significant, but they can be overcome. We all need access and skills, but we also need to make sure they're truly useful and meaningful for everyone, and that they provide what we all need to thrive. The 2009 Pew Internet & American Life "Home Broadband Adoption" report showed that half of all users who either are on dial-up connections or don't have home Internet access at all question the relevance of the Internet in their lives, for example.[40] We can't make change without everyone on board, and if we don't fix the existing structures soon, we'll continue to replicate and reinforce social hierarchies that have been constraining us for far too long.

The process of breaking down those structures, however, starts with you. As we'll discuss in the next chapter, sharing works only if you—YOU—participate in the conversation.

3   We Are What You Share

YOUR PARTICIPATION in social media is much more than just the individual bits you choose to share. As the online universe expands and merges with our offline lives, a whole ecosystem has emerged. Each of us has a role in that new environment, whether or not we're aware of it, and what we choose to do with our roles ultimately will make or break the health of the social networking ecosystem.

Within that ecosystem, a number of elements are required to keep it in good health: generosity, identity, empathy, and authenticity. When one or more of these are lacking from your participation (how you share), the overall picture of what you're about suffers, as does your ability to influence others and make change. Furthermore, your opportunity to discover and learn more about yourself diminishes as well.

Trading in Karma

Within social networks, an economy is at work, but it's not based on money. It is instead a *gift economy*. Simply put, people who participate in this kind of system believe that it's a good idea to do good things, regardless of any quantifiable return on their investment. According to Wikipedia—a fabulous example of a gift economy—this do-gooder system embraces a culture in which

> valuable goods and services are regularly given without any *explicit* agreement for immediate or future rewards (i.e. there is no formal *quid pro quo*). Ideally, simultaneous or recurring giving serves to circulate and redistribute valuables within the community.[1]

In technology, the gift economy is most obvious in the open source movement.[2] Software developers make code available to everyone to use and/or improve upon, with no monetary compensation. The understanding among open source participants is that no one of us is smarter than a group of people working to solve a problem, and we all benefit when that problem has been solved.

Early adopters of social media tools were technology folks accustomed to participating in gift economies, either through open source or Creative Commons[3] licensing (which gives authors control over how their work is used, if at all, by others). Popular social network and media tools such as Twitter, Facebook, and MySpace are not open source (they are applications whose code is private and owned by for-profit businesses), but the spirit of community enhancement and problem solving is widespread among users. That community-based culture grew out of the way in which early adopters—tech-savvy people—encouraged open source principles, such as share and share alike, always include the name of the person who provided the information and/or its source, and support others by responding to requests for advice and guidance.

Social media's facilitation of sharing, connecting, and storytelling creates a perfect stage for extending the gift economy to everyone. And within this economy, we measure our own participation through social capital. In simplest terms, think of social capital as karma: When you do good things, good things come back to you.

This arrangement is not *explicit*; there is no set of standards such as "Do X, and Y will happen." Many of us, especially Americans, find it hard to wrap our heads around trading information or services without some kind of defined payback, since our grounding in market-based economies encourages us to think of everything in terms of direct transactions. If I pay you $5, you'll give me a pint of Ben and Jerry's. If I refinish your flooring, you'll pay me for my labor. Even when we think of bartering, we still focus on the transactional moment: If I cook you dinner, you'll show me how to set up a Web site.

In the gift economy, transactions aren't viewed on a one-to-one basis; a collection of actions over time is what establishes a person's social capital. That holistic view of what people's actions say about them contributes to the overall health of the social media ecosystem. What kinds of actions and assets make someone valuable? Tara Hunt, author of *The Whuffie Factor: Using the Power of Social Networks to Build Your Business* (Crown Business, 2009), presented six factors at a Women Who Tech panel discussion.[4] I'm giving her key terms, followed by my interpretations of her definitions:

Connections: Who do you know? Not just important or famous people, either. Are you connected to lots of different kinds of people who can complete different tasks?

Reputation: What are you known for? What do people say about your expertise?

Influence: Can you move groups of people, small or large, to take some action?

Access to ideas, talent: Beyond your own skill set, do you have ways of reaching out to others with talent and knowledge?

Access to resources: You may not be able to fund a particular project, but do you know people who can? Do you have ways of generating physical support?

Potential access: Will your access to resources and talent stay static in the future, or will it continue to grow?

Saved-up favors: We're not writing down every good deed, but do people remember you for the ways that you help others? Your own generosity is incredibly important. Is your goodwill with your social capital part of your reputation?

Accomplishments: What awards have you won? What concrete recognition—papers or articles published, etc.— have you received for your work?

All of the facets of your social capital together make up your net worth in the gift economy.

As you accumulate social capital, you spend it, reinvest it, and accumulate more. What follows is an example of a social capital growth cycle; keep in mind, though, that it's generally much bigger than this Y-follows-X example. It's an ecosystem, not a linear argument.

Let's say Julie is well known in her social circle as an expert on craft beer. It's a great hobby, and every time she samples a new beer, she posts a short review as a status update on Facebook, which leads to lively discussions in the comments section with her friends. Having conversations is how she builds her *reputation*.

Friends know that she's a microbrew aficionado, so they post links to her Facebook profile, pointing to new beer releases and brewpubs. She takes time to thank them and lets them know later if she checked them out. Thanking her friends and responding to their posts also builds her *reputation*, because we all like to be appreciated, right?

Those folks start sharing her reviews with other microbrew fans, and those fans ask to be Julie's friend on Facebook so that they can read her information firsthand. When she accepts new friend requests, she's building her *connections* and her *access*. A few months into this process, Julie finds out about a microbrew festival near her town that is accepting nominations for judges. She asks the people interested in her beer posts to vote for her (using some of her *saved-up favors*). When she wins a spot, she offers to host a local microbrew meet-up at the festival, which puts goodwill back into the system, and it also helps get the word out about the festival. Her social capital increases.

While I'm sure that every one of you has expertise to release into the world, it's not necessary to specialize in one thing. If you're known in your social circles as a go-to person for help, guidance, or advice, you'll flourish in social media. If you're not (yet), these tools make establishing expertise incredibly easy. They're built to help us operate in the gift economy effectively and efficiently.

Be careful, however, of exploiting the gift economy—either purposefully *or* accidentally. Doing so can make you a pretty bad social capitalist; you don't want to be the ExxonMobil of social capitalism. You've probably already experienced good social capitalists and bad social capitalists in your daily wanderings throughout the digital world. Think about a listserv or e-mail group you belong to and some of the participants there. Let's say you belong to a group devoted to baking. How do you feel about the members who share interesting links to articles with healthy substitution tips, or who answer questions about ingredients, or who just generally move the conversation along? Now think about the people who consistently post pictures of their own cookies, or who ask for advice but who never answer questions, or who consistently drive the conversation back to their own kitchens. . . . You sense the difference, yes?

The same is true with these emerging tools—it's hard to build out a network with a bunch of one-way dead-ends. Humans gravitate toward people and groups who are supportive and who aren't (entirely) self-centered. In the online version of that gravitation instinct, it's easier than ever to find those people.

What's critical to understand is that the behavior we're seeing in these online communities is not that much different from what we see offline. Each of us has been working with social capital all along, but now that we have tools like Facebook and Twitter that map and document our social interactions, our social capital is much more transparent.

It's not just clearer to *us* how we're interacting with other people, but it's also more obvious to *those around us* what each of us has to offer and how we operate. Jessica Clark, research director for American University's Center for Social Media, says that she had been studying the role of social networking tools in politics for a while, but she didn't really understand their power for everyday life until she met Alex Hillman in 2007.[5] Hillman, a Philadelphia-based web developer, helped cofound Independents Hall, a "coworking" space where freelancers can rent desks so that they don't have to work in isolation at home or in coffee shops.[6] "The whole vibe of Indy Hall was open source—the assumption was that shared space would lead to useful information sharing and creative collaboration," Clark observes. Hillman himself conducts much of his life online, enthusiastically sharing both personal and professional information via Twitter, blogs, and discussion lists. "His energy and openness was infectious; it offered inspiration to open yourself up and see what you could give back to communities that you're part of," she noted.

Displaying trust, kindness, and empathy—all values that social capital and the gift economy are based on—has never been easier, or more important.

On the Internet, Everybody Knows You're a Dog

Thanks to social networks' transparency, it's also more important, and more accepted, to use your real name and identity. Identity is a key component of your work in the ecosystem. When you act anonymously, your reach is limited because you're not leaving a record of your actions. When you participate publicly, your actions leave a public trail. It's still fine in some cases to build your relationships and social capital under a pseudonym (and there are a few cases where it's necessary). As divisions between online and offline life dissolve, however, it has become much more valuable to combine many of your identities into one powerhouse.

Contributing our opinions and experiences to public conversations using our real identities plants a stake in the ground, and on the public record, wherever it may be kept, that validates the identities we create for ourselves online. We're still getting used to the idea of using our real names and pictures—it wasn't that long ago that no one ever did that, and anonymity was all the rage—but by doing so, we're able to use our identities to create trust with one another. When we trust the people with whom we're sharing details of our lives or opinions, we build collective empathy. It's easier to trust a person online with a real name attached to a screen name, a picture instead of an icon, and a running log of the person's interests and comments. That trust and empathy creates the building blocks for wider change, as we'll see later in this chapter.

We arrived at this juncture of identity and trust as a result of gradual adoption of Internet technologies in our daily lives. But in the early 1990s, it was widely popular to claim that everyone online could pretend to be anything they wanted. The famous 1993 *New Yorker* cartoon by Peter Steiner featuring two dogs chatting about Internet identity ("On the Internet, nobody knows you're a dog") pretty much sums up the ethic: We can all hide behind the giant curtain of technology.

The Internet removed physical constraints that our silly human bodies put on us, as well as all kinds of social mores that prevented us from saying and doing what we wanted. But creating an online identity was still the purview of nerds and geeks back then. By the mid-'90s, more people were joining discussion lists and chat rooms, but mostly under assumed identities, with clever nicknames that represented slices of their identities—GiantsFan4Ever or KnitterManiac2002. Sometimes the nicknames represented more private desires and alter egos.

In 1995, during my college fangrrl days listening to the Barenaked Ladies (a band. Canadian. Humourous, with an extra Canadian *u*!), I became a regular participant in the BNL channel on Internet Relay Chat protocol, or IRC.[7] The online chat service came out in 1988, making it one of the oldest online communication services in the book. My nickname, to the best of my recollection, was "deannabanana." It was what my friends called me in jest; I felt like it was close enough to who I was but eased me out of the scary step of Revealing A Last Name.

By the early 2000s, more people were comfortable with using their real names, but privacy and security concerns remained. Never before had we experienced such unfettered access to other people's lives, and no one knew exactly how it was going to play out. People were concerned with being "outed" in one way or another, so we still concealed the more personal and quirky parts of our lives. It was not socially acceptable, for example, to attach hobbies to one's public identity. Letting people know that you were a fan of a sci-fi series or that you obsessed nightly over Japanese garden design was not necessarily a good thing.

As the Internet evolved, and as more people started using it for different purposes, some of the fear around revealing different parts of oneself lessened. Purchasing products online, for example, required a new level of trust when giving out credit card information and mailing addresses. Susan Mernit, a web strategist and founder of Oakland Local, suggests that online shopping especially helped build trust in the Great Big Ether: People gave their credit card numbers and addresses to systems online, and, largely, nothing *bad* happened to them.[8] Additionally, businesses went to great lengths to ensure that people had a safe shopping experience and maintained control over their identities and how much personal information they wanted to share.[9]

Our willingness to use our names is also accelerating a trend toward more authenticity. Sharing every last tidbit isn't required (or even desirable), but there's more opportunity to share information that previously might have been saved just for people we already know. We belong to numerous social circles—work, politics, hobbies, sports, religion, school, neighborhood—and now that everyone's lives are overlapping, the overlap is OK because it's happening to all of us at the same time.

If I were seeking to meet other BNL fans today, I wouldn't necessarily search for a dedicated fan site. I'd start with an online social network I already belong to, like Facebook, and join a BNL fan page or group. The online network is already in place, and, more important, people's identities are already validated by these networks. We are already participating as ourselves. No more "deannabanana" hanging out in the chat room; now it's Deanna Zandt joining the fan page or friending the band.

Engaging with one another online has the wider cultural benefit of inspiring more civic engagement offline. Studies show that young people who participate in online communities are more likely to take part in *offline* civic activities later in life. This is the case even when their online interactions are purely social or for enjoyment (such as joining a Barenaked Ladies fan site). Even in these spaces, teens are developing real skills, including learning how to assess and share information.[10]

Using your real name yields many benefits, starting with social capital. By associating your knowledge, opinions, and sense of humor with your real identity, you're helping to build a profile of who you are. Many social networks get indexed by search engines like Google, so your posts will come up when people search for you or the topics you're posting about. (Of course, you will still want to keep some things private, which you can do by investigating and adjusting your privacy settings.)

Developments in online security and privacy, as well as the normalization of a variety of Internet activities—such as on-line shopping, chat, and social network participation—have reached a point where folks are becoming comfortable with revealing parts of themselves. And our values are inherent in those activities we participate in, from the overtly political, like joining a Facebook Cause that all of our friends can see, to the more subtle, like complaining about working two jobs and still not having health care. Everything we choose to share doesn't just represent those individual events, but also contributes to the larger picture of what our values and experiences are.

Those contributions create trust between the members of any given network, and the combination of high trust and valid identities enhances the depth, breadth, and overall health of the social media ecosystem. We start to share more of what's important to us (as we'll see in the next section), and through the trust we create with our real identities, we foster empathy and understanding.

Your Life Makes History
••••••••••••••••••••

Besides being beneficial to you and building your social capital, sharing yourself and your life experiences is a highly political act.

Remember that old adage, "The personal is political"? It's never been truer than at this moment. Each bit of information that we share with others becomes, collectively, an act of political significance. "Politics" is not just about candidates, elections, and ballot initiatives. Politics is the art and science of influencing or changing any kind of power relationship: the cultural norms by which we act; the laws that govern us; the expectations we experience based on our gender, race, class, sexuality, abilities, and more. When I talk about political work, I'm talking about challenging and radically redefining those power relationships, using the tools that social networks provide.

It's easy to point to the "what I had for breakfast" phenomenon and decry social media as nothing more than a narcissistic endeavor. I understand where the impetus to dismiss the posting of these minutiae comes from—certainly no one should be terribly interested in the details of our daily lives, not when read as individual events. It's the bigger picture those events make up that is so exciting.

Step with me into the Wayback Machine for a minute, to a supposedly simpler time when behavior was neatly compartmentalized: the 1950s. Now, I wasn't alive during that time, but I've seen enough of those "health and hygiene" movies to know what the deal was.[11] Using the '50s as a metaphor, let's compare Then and Now.

During that time, men worked, and their work stayed in the work sphere. Upper- and middle-class women stayed home and took care of the kids, heading up the domestic sphere. Publicly, white men were in charge of just about everything: government, media, and other public domains. There was little crossover between spheres, and anyone who didn't fit the prescribed white, heterosexual model was denied a voice.

I think we can safely say that this was one of the most repressed times in American history.

Fast-forward to the rip-roarin' times of social media. It's no longer a requirement, in most cases, to keep work and personal lives separate. With the advent of mobile, always-on technology, it's sort of impossible. As people take part in social media, different parts of their lives start to manifest in a more public way.

Look at any of your friends' Facebook or MySpace profiles, and you'll see a pretty wide swath of things they're interested in (music, movies, what have you), as well as causes and social/political situations they care about based on what they've listed in their interests, or what groups they belong to, or what they're a fan of. With whatever we share, we are saying that we trust the people around us with this information. And, in most cases, that trust is rewarded, as people in our communities show, in various direct and indirect ways, their support for what we share. By showing support, we each become trustworthy to one another—all of which builds our social capital and leads to pipelines of empathy and understanding. This, of course, assumes that people are fundamentally good, trustworthy people. I'm hopeful they are,[12] and that hope is a fundamental principle driving my work for change.

Empathy—the ability not just to have concern for, but to *share* another person's emotions—develops when we participate in each other's lives. Prior to social network technology, it was difficult to stay loosely connected to a large number of people, and thus difficult to have much empathy for people outside of our tightly knit groups. In early Internet social settings, such as forums, anonymity fueled bad behavior and ultimately distrust.

Now that relationships and trust influence how we receive and manage digital information, we're becoming more connected, and thus we have the capacity to be more empathetic. That trust-created empathy will lead us away from the isolation and resulting apathy that we've experienced as a culture, arising from the 20th century's focus on mass communications and market demographics.

Here's a story about how building trust through social networks has worked for me. A couple of years ago, I spoke at a conference in northern California. After my song and dance, Leif Utne, the vice president of community development for the software company Zanby, came up to introduce himself. He was working on a project that he wanted to get my employer, Jim Hightower, involved with. We exchanged contact info and became Facebook friends; later we started following each other on Twitter.

About a year and a half later, Leif messaged me to say that he was coming to Brooklyn for a visit and wanted to know if I'd like to get coffee. Sure! Of course! When we sat down a few days later, I asked him how the baby was—he and his wife had spent a long time adopting a baby from Guatemala, and Leif had even lived there for ten months. He lit up and showed me recent photos, and then asked how my dog, Izzy, was adjusting to life in Brooklyn. I had adopted her from a rescue organization, and we laughed at how the processes for adopting dogs and children were eerily similar.

Leif asked if he could show me a new online service that he'd taken a job with, one that would give groups a way to connect their memberships. Absolutely, I said. We did a run-through, and he talked about some of his company's successes. I started thinking of clients who could really use something like this tool and offered to put him in touch with them.

My online friendship with Leif is significant for several reasons. Social media enabled a kind of "identity authentication" between us. I was aware of Leif's family's work with the *Utne Reader* before I met him, but being connected via social media gave me insight into some of his values and interests. And vice versa. More important, though, it allowed us to collect seemingly unrelated fragments of information about one another over time, and to create a wide-angled picture of the other person with those fragments. Technology writer Clive Thompson calls this phenomenon "ambient awareness" of the people around us.[13]

It doesn't impact my life at all to know that Leif is heading to the airport, and he probably doesn't care that I spent an extra 30 minutes with my dog in the park this morning. But over time, we are able to see a portrait of one another's lives take shape and feel connected. While Leif's trip to the airport doesn't affect my daily life, if he misses his plane, I feel bad for him. There's the empathy, simply by being aware of another person's "mundane" activities. Our portraits of one another facilitated an in-person conversation that otherwise would have been stilted and awkward:

"So, you, uh, have kids?"

"No, you?"

"Yeah, one. A little boy."

"Uh-huh."

Instead, we were able to tap into what we care about pretty quickly, and the landing into the "business" end of the meeting was much smoother.

Admittedly, experimenting with what it means to share different parts of our lives can sometimes be uncomfortable. Chip Conley, the CEO of a family of boutique hotels in northern California called Joie de Vivre,[14] offers a case in point. In 2009, he wrote about the fallout from photos he posted to Facebook from his latest Burning Man[15] trip. Some workers were surprised to see Conley in a tutu and a sarong.[16] The complicated part wasn't that he didn't want them online, or that his investors or board members didn't want them online; it was that some employees struggled with seeing their fearless leader show a carefree side of himself that didn't "fit" with the standard work environment. We're all still determining what we each individually consider acceptable amounts of information, as well as what we'll tolerate organizationally and culturally.

Thanks to the alienating effect of mass communications, our ability to converse directly with one another, and to engage with the larger culture in a meaningful way, has withered. While no one has figured out a precise formula for what amount or mix of sharing creates empathy, presenting real pictures of real lives indisputably frees us from our pigeonholes. Social networks give us the opportunity to reengage with *one another*.

Diving In

Before we float along in too much theory, let's discuss some concrete tactics for sharing. Many people who are just starting out have trouble deciding what to post. A flat-out easy beginner's guidepost comes from the illustrious Susan Mernit, who once told participants in a workshop we cotaught: "If you're wondering whether you should post something or not, you probably shouldn't."

The genesis of this axiom comes from a key principle of social networks: Authenticity rules. Again, the idea is not to share everything under the sun, but to make meaningful connections based on the substance of who we really are. Social media "gurus" and "mavens" often slip "authenticity" into smarmy marketing blog posts. Ignore them. They are not the guides you are looking for. But authenticity is.

My cousin Cheryl is a therapist in Washington, DC, and she told me about the stereo equalizer model of relationship intimacy. Reliability, trust, availability, etc., are the main components—skew one of those bands outta whack, and the whole mix is off.

Social media authenticity works much the same way. It's a mix of personal insights, professional announcements, expertise (whether about a job or a hobby), passion, lots of opinion, and humor. It takes some experimentation to figure out what mix sounds right to you.

Authenticity is a mix of different elements.

The experimentation is why Susan's advice is so dead-on: What you perceive to be good, what *you* feel comfortable with, that's what people will pick up on as they share in your experiences.

For people who are largely private folks who don't want to tell the world about the silly stuff their kid just did, *that's fine.* Share your impressions of an article related to your work. You don't have to use your most conversational voice, either. You can maintain a fairly professional tone (though do try not to be emotionless) and still come across as engaging and insightful. The mix is what's going to make your voice sound good—to you and to others.

For some people, it's easy to share personal news and events. Me, I have no bones about tweeting funny things my mom says, details of a party, or (loads of) pictures of my dog. It's a way for me to keep a running log of things that are important to me. That said, my guidepost is to not share things that would make me feel vulnerable, like details of my dating life. I share information once in a while about my health, either to reach out for help or to show solidarity with others, but I consciously keep it to a minimum—simply because that's what feels right to me.

The experimentation can be uncomfortable to start with, but know that it's OK to make mistakes here and there; social media is quite a bit more forgiving (and forgetful) than more traditional forms of media (and, I would add, also more forgiving than blogging).

Worried about it all being Out There? Jaclyn Friedman, an author and coeditor of *Yes Means Yes!*, made a great point in a workshop I was leading about how our perception of social media is rapidly changing, similar to how our perception of tattoos has changed in the last 50 years. Think about the attitudes toward a person who got a tattoo in 1960, versus attitudes now. It's the same with social media. Ten years ago, someone getting a swig of TMI[17] via Google search results might have had an adverse reaction. Today, seeing something a little off-topic in a Twitter stream is not as big of a deal.

That said, I do want to mention that some folks are in jobs where more attention needs to be paid to privacy and security (you know who you are). Different parameters are in play when working on establishing your mix, but you shouldn't keep yourself out of social media altogether. Almost all of us are already represented online. Ever try Googling yourself? Social media sites generally appear within the top 10 search results; you should do your best to influence how you appear, even if it's to show that you're largely a private person.

How Sharing Inspires Social Change
••••••••••••••••••••••••••••

When we share who we are—what life is *really* like for most of us—we are committing small political acts. We all receive cues from the culture(s) around us to indicate how we should act, based on our gender, or our sexual identity, or our race. Often those cues are biased and stereotypical, and don't represent the reality of our identity. When we share snippets and nuanced insights, we have the opportunity to reject those prescribed expectations and to share the real deal with others. That exposure to other people's thoughts and opinions is almost like a new version of consciousness-raising for the digital age.

Consciousness-raising is an example of how sharing our experiences and rejecting cultural expectations has worked on behalf of social change in the past. For younger folks (like me) who might not know what it is, consciousness-raising was a big part of the U.S. feminist movement in the late 1960s and early 1970s. Many women were experiencing social oppression in isolation. And if these experiences remained individual and isolated, it would be difficult, if not impossible, to organize a movement to change them. Many women were not involved in the participatory politics that were so popular at the time, and some found traditional models of organizing off-putting.

Thus arose this idea that women—mostly white, middle-class women, that is—could get together in small groups in their towns and cities, and speak freely ("rap," no joke) about aspects of their lives that they found difficult or troubling. Other women in the room found commonality with those experiences, and soon everyone would (hopefully) become conscious that there was a systemic problem that extended beyond their own lives. The realization of widespread struggle would (again, hopefully) lead to political action and involvement, often through more traditional structures.

This model wasn't without problems—as mentioned, consciousness-raising was popular among middle-class white women, which marginalized the voices of women of color and queer women. (We'll talk more in chapter 5 about how online consciousness-raising can also have a marginalizing effect if we're not careful.) Put simply, though, we see that sharing personal experiences has a profound effect on social change. The Not In Our Town[18] project, for example, started out as a documentary film to address how the citizens of Billings, Montana, banded together to address hate crimes that had happened in their midst. It has evolved into a full-fledged national movement built on the power of storytelling against hate. Sharing our stories matters. If I'm posting grumblings about pay problems at my job, and someone else in my workplace sees that and responds, that could be the beginning of labor organizing for that company. If I see people celebrating the passage of marriage equality laws in their home state, it might inspire me to find out what's happening in mine.

The result is not always a clear path of inspiration to direct action, but the shifts in consciousness can make a profound difference in how we and our contacts interpret and respond to issues. Moreover, we can create overlapping public conversations between groups of people that otherwise in the past might have remained isolated from one another, thanks to the racial, class, and gender divisions our society has in place.

An incident that occurred during the summer of 2009 offers an illuminating example of how overlapping social spaces online can support change efforts. A private country club in Philadelphia banned a group of African-American children from swimming in its pool, even though the kids' camp had paid for their swimming privileges.[19] Capturing the public's shock and outrage, comedian Elon James White, host of the popular web series "This Week in Blackness," opened an episode with the words: "Hi, I'm broadcasting live from 1952 . . ."[20]

Social networks lit up with discussions of the incident. Acting on simple moral outrage is a start, but when everyday people contributed their own histories of childhood discrimination, much more fundamentally painful and ultimately consciousness-shifting, deeper work began.

When I heard about the incident, I signed petitions, I passed the info along on Twitter and Facebook, and I talked about it with my friends, both online and off. As the dialogue continued, people started to share stories on Twitter and Facebook about the first time they had been discriminated against. I read story after unfiltered, unedited story, written by friends. The stories were devastating; so was the fact that I hadn't heard them before.

I realized that without social media, I probably never would have heard those stories. Or I might have heard one of them, isolated from others. Being white, I have never been a victim of racism, and because many of my friends are white, they haven't either. Before the emergence of social media, I most likely wouldn't have found myself in the company of a group of people of color sharing their childhood discrimination stories so openly and honestly.

To share that kind of intimacy requires some sort of explicit or assumed "safe space"—a forum of sorts, where one can express views without threat of abuse or harassment. Safe space requires a tremendous amount of trust, and that trust allowed the people sharing the stories with each other to extend the conversation past the sound bite moments that get played out in media and other traditional public forums. "Usually when people of color talk publicly, it's about our feelings, our mistakes, and being frank about our shortcomings," says Ludovic Blain, director of the Progressive Era Project and a longtime social justice activist. "Often when white folks speak in the same setting, it's about their initiatives and how they'll make it right. That's perverted. In the case of the racist pool, the scene was the same: people of color discussing heart-wrenching issues in front of whites. But those people were also doing a rare thing—publicly discussing what whites had done wrong."[21] The empathy based on shared experience, combined with trust that the conversation would be productive, brought this moment to a more necessarily intense place.

Additionally, people decided to share their stories for many reasons: to release a painful memory and get it off their chests, to connect with others who had experienced similar racism as children, to potentially educate those who needed to hear their memories, and more. Thus, the voyeuristic aspect of the experience was strong. My whiteness was hidden for a moment (via my silence, not sharing a common past experience), and social networks allowed me to enter a conversation that otherwise might have been altered by my presence. I was able to benefit regardless of whether the sharers intended for me to, and that cultural voyeurism needs to be clear when discussing issues that deal with bias around race, gender, class, and other kinds of privilege.

Social networks facilitate overlap among groups that previously had no opportunity to engage in dialogue. Even though humans will always be drawn to others who they think are like them in one way or another, sharing powerful stories with one other has the potential to reach across social boundaries and create new kinds of safe spaces. Safe spaces have traditionally been organized around identities and experiences—women's groups, ethnicity-centric groups, queer groups, etc. Now we'll have the opportunity to create new criteria for trust that will ultimately contribute to new safe spaces.

I received an education that day. It's one thing to read stories in the newspaper and get upset; it's an entirely different, deeper experience to read the words of friends and colleagues sharing intimate, painful moments in real time. Those shared moments left me feeling not just more passionate about addressing racism, but also more willing to hear what's being said when I need to listen.

Change does not, and will not, happen in isolation or on an individual basis—we need each other to produce results. As we start to explore with social media, we have the potential to deepen our understanding of one another's life experiences, and of ourselves. Telling our stories in real, authentic ways becomes critical to moving others toward progress and change.

Authenticity, the Great Equalizer

We've figured out, then, that shared experience is a fundamental building block for social change movements, and that social media makes sharing experiences, as author Clay Shirky puts it, "ridiculously easy." But it's not enough to put random things out there. What you share in social networks needs to come from a real place in your personality: your own experiences, opinions, hopes, and fears. It's those authentic tidbits that are going to create connections of empathy and trust with other people, and ultimately create an antidote to the narcissism and political apathy that mainstream culture has pushed us toward.

Let's discuss for a moment the nature of the authentic self. Many people I've spoken with are questioning whether participation in social media is a performance. And if it is, does that mean it's any less authentic? My opinion is that yes, it is a performance. But so is writing this book. And so was the conversation I had with my mom earlier this evening. And so was the casual hello I said to my neighbor this morning.

In short, everything we do outside of ourselves is some sort of performance. We have myriad rumblings inside our brains at any giving moment, but before our thoughts become words and actions, we initiate an often-unconscious series of deliberations about what we choose to do. That's filtering ourselves at a basic level and creating some sort of "performance." So, let's look at that word differently. Bob Holman, poet and proprietor of New York's Bowery Poetry Club, asked me to reconsider the definition of "performance" that I'm using. "We think about 'performance' as something that's planned and rehearsed, which somehow makes it less authentic to us," he said. "But what if we thought about 'performance' like how we apply it to cars, or horses? How we then judge performance changes radically."[22]

In other words, let's not think about performance as something planned, practiced, and thus potentially inauthentic (because everything we do is planned at some level—"planned" is not a measure of authenticity); rather, let's frame performance as an experience whose quality we can determine by thinking about how well—how authentically, perhaps—the experience worked for us. Did the performance touch us emotionally? Did it engage us to take action? How are we different now that we've shared that experience with other people?

If we go with this new definition of performance, we no longer question whether our posts are "real" or "rehearsed." The real point is quality: How "good" are we at expressing our true selves? If our networks feel that we are presenting ourselves authentically, then we have succeeded.

How authentic we are to the people around us matters more than ever. In a thriving social network ecosystem, increased amounts of authenticity are another important ingredient. It's not enough to just present your identity and hope for the best; people connect to one another when they feel trust, and authenticity is a key component toward building trust.

Know Your Network, Know Yourself

Authentic interactions with one another also provide us with a way to explore and make connections in the social ecosystem in entirely new ways, as we share experiences and perceptions about how the world operates. In the past, we were passive receivers of information. Because of the way mass communications are structured, we've had to be shunted into giant demographic bins, and as a result, our feelings of isolation have increased.

The trajectory we're following is a little terrifying if we just look at mass media as an indicator of cultural health—one could devote an entire book alone to the specter of reality television and the psychology behind all those tryouts.[23]

But sneaking up to save us from that blight are social networks: Sharing our *authentic* selves, versus projecting some *spectacle* of ourselves, holds opportunities to explore each other's identities, and thus gain a greater understanding of our needs and values. Through authenticity, we experience understanding, and we create the empathy needed to maintain a healthy social network ecosystem.

Looking back, we've been dealing with a sense of increasing isolation over the past century, in part due to the (largely white) flight from cities to the suburbs, and in part due to how mass media have treated us as faceless consumers of product. We're deluged with mass messages—we're exposed to about 2,000 pieces of advertising per day. One way out of the cacophony of mass media is to figure out a way to be recognized. But recognition is pretty limited in our culture; one of the few avenues is to become famous. Michael Wesch, a professor of anthropology at Kansas State University, talked about the cultural isolation of the last century in an address delivered at the 2009 Personal Democracy Forum conference (I highly recommend watching the online video). "When the conversations of the culture are happening on television, it's a one-way conversation. You have to be on TV to have a voice, you have to be on TV to be significant," he said.[24] Before the reality TV craze, most of us couldn't achieve fame without large amounts of luck and talent. Reality

TV changed all that. Suddenly we could become famous just by *showing up*. It didn't matter that we'd make fools of ourselves; we'd be *recognized*, and thus valued . . . even if only for 15 minutes or less.

The onslaught of social media started to move people away from broadcasting inauthentic experiences, led first by the blogging crowd. Blogs are often associated with electoral and advocacy politics, but in practice, the blogging community is much larger and more diverse. Many bloggers are pure diarists, keeping logs of their daily lives and experiences. The rise of other types of social media services that enabled people to contribute short status updates exponentially added to this grand logging experiment. The collective process of posting status updates, pictures, video, blog entries, reviews, and recommendations is called *lifestreaming*.

There are two sides to the lifestreaming coin: the narcissistic and the self-defining. Narcissism is the easy road: *Look at me, look at what I do, look how deserving I am of this attention—and I don't care what anyone else thinks.* The best example of narcissism can be found in the lengths that people go to in reality TV. It's not just money they're after. It's also the huge amount of attention being showered on them. Their inauthenticity is palpable, and their contribution toward cultural and social advancement is low. We experience these people on social networks as well—remember those bad social capitalists from earlier in the chapter, who only broadcast and don't share?

The flip side of this coin is the movement toward using social network tools to engage in a process of self-definition. We're all searching for recognition in our culture, but rather than using spectacle to validate our existence, we can use our relationships, and the trust we build as a result of sharing, to pursue this path of self-exploration. We can't find that on our own; we need each other to evaluate our experiences and then validate our identities. Canadian philosopher Charles Taylor agrees that the search for one's self can't happen in isolation.[25] Even hermits who run off to the mountains are in some sort of conversation—with God, with their "inner self," with nature, or with whomever/whatever. Humans *need* to be in dialogue. "We are expected to develop our own opinions, outlook, stances to things, to a considerable degree through solitary reflection," says Taylor. "But this is not how things work with important issues. . . . We define this always in dialogue with, sometimes in struggle against, the identities [those around us] want to recognize in us." Sharing on social networks can be of great assistance in the search for ourselves, because so much of what happens there *is* dialogue. What you share with others creates the space where conversation can happen; and your experiences, as you use the tools to explore your identity, can start to effect change.

Remember how we discussed the fact that a big part of our social capital is reputation and our contributions to the gift economy? People who share information and answer questions, who create connections of empathy and trust, all while building their own social capital, offer the greatest potential to shift our culture away from the pending implosion of narcissism and apathy that mass communications have created.

Our ability to use social networks and media—by reaching inside for understanding and reaching out beyond oneself to interact with purpose—can help us to lay out the building blocks for change. But there are still barriers to the utopian super-fun happy land of the Internet. Your presence is required, but so is your willingness to take risks to break down those roadblocks.

4   Trust Everyone

WHO DO YOU TRUST?

Why?

Maybe you just said to yourself, "Wait, who do I trust for what? I trust different people for different things." That's right, you do—and our sharing on social networks is changing how we assign trust, or authority, to different people and organizations. In this transitional moment, as we're not just sharing what's important to us and what's on our agendas but also looking at how we measure the success of our work and our expertise, we can radically redefine what authority means to us and who becomes influential.

When we think about "authority," we generally conjure up images of cops, teachers, bosses, legislators. They are the People In Charge. In traditional power systems, those with more influence or power (a relatively small number, given how many of us are on the planet altogether) are dependent on our being passive consumers of information. We're freed significantly from that dependency when we're given easy tools with which to share our stories.

When people have access to low-cost, user-friendly tools for self-expression, everyone becomes an expert at something.[1]

Thanks to social network technologies, how we determine authority—whom we trust for what—is rapidly changing the face of culture and politics. When we share our own and others' experiences and opinions, we can begin to overhaul traditional power dynamics and relationships. We start to determine for ourselves what's relevant and important, and subvert the institutions that seek to keep the status quo.

That doesn't mean that there aren't challenges to the floodgates opening—information overload threatens the sanity of many, and we're not well equipped (yet) to process everything that's coming at us in productive, responsible ways. Nonetheless, the release of information from hierarchical constraints creates the opportunity to redistribute the centers of power and authority that have long controlled our cultural information sources.

The Anatomy of Organic Authority

We have, of course, been sharing opinions with each other since the beginning of time. What makes this moment so unique? The speed by which we share information, the number of people we share it with, and our potential—individually and collectively—to wield as much influence as established experts and institutions.

We're used to having institutions tell us what's interesting, important, and relevant. Take movie reviews, for example: How often do you look up reviews before you get to the theater? We do this because we want to know more about the film, and reviewers and critics have titles and status. Baratunde Thurston,[2] comedian and web editor for the *Onion* and host of *Popular Science*'s *Future Of* television show, calls that status we assign "institutional authority"—we can point to specific reasons why we trust the authority of those prominent sources.

Another kind of authority is at work, and that's the trust we have in our social connections—our friends, colleagues, and family members, for example—to pass on information that's relevant and interesting. (And we ourselves have authority on a variety of subjects; as we discussed in chapter 3, we use our social capital to build and share this authority in social networks, both online and off.) Relying on our social networks for information creates what Thurston calls "organic authority." It grows over time and is dependent on more idiosyncratic variables.

If a friend with whom you've seen movies for the last 10 years said, "You should see *When Harry Met Sally*. You'd love it," you would consider her previous recommendations and whether you trust her advice on movies. If a work colleague recommended a movie, you'd go through a similar process, but maybe you'd weigh his opinion differently from the opinion of your 10-year movie partner. Now think about that movie review in the newspaper: Is the reviewer's opinion more valuable than the friend's or colleague's? Probably not. Chances are, it just has a *different* value.

Institutional Authority on the Hot Seat
••••••••••••••••••••••••••••••••

Traditionally, folks higher up in the food chain have advised us on what we should eat and drink (and where to do it if dining out), which celebrity we should pay the most attention to, who's the smartest politician in the room,[3] and which laws are bad and which are good. All of this advice comes from, as Jim Hightower says, the Powers That Be, instead of the Powers That Ought To Be.[4]

Social networks threaten the order of things in the scheme of institutional authority. Online, our connections and relationships are mapped for all to see, which makes sharing authority easy, and what we share is generally visible to all. Instead of relying solely on what these institutions define for the world around us and being asked to trust that they know what's best, we can now turn to social networking tools to establish and verify our own and others' authority. Instead of trusting a select few, we're using our own measurements and value systems to determine what's relevant and important to us.

When we make up our own minds about what's important and what's not important is maddening to most of the institutions around us, which depend on our reliance on their institutional authority. It's turning a whole lot of institutions—businesses, legislative bodies, traditional media—upside down. And they're not taking it well. In late 2009, for example, Rupert Murdoch threatened to remove all of News Corporation's content from being indexed by Google, which would effectively block people's ability to organically discover news and content from the media colossus. Over in the land of music sharing, for years the Recording Industry Association of America (RIAA)[5] has been notorious for chasing down people who share files online, instead of embracing the idea that sharing promotes sales rather than discouraging them.[6] Knowing they're facing this kind of resistance is a hard pill for many organizations to swallow. But in this emerging world order, the more that organizations of any kind continue to insist they know best, the worse off they'll be. People are embracing the idea that they have a certain amount of control and influence over what they do with the information that comes their way, and they will increasingly resist and reject organizations that don't embrace this ethos with them.

Institutional authority won't disappear altogether, at least not anytime soon. Social networks, however, with their basis in relationships, have a hard time tolerating the old demands of one-to-many messaging—"This is what's good for you, and you'll just have to trust us."

Actually, we *don't* just have to trust you anymore. We've got a network of complementary, organic authorities to verify or discredit what you're putting out there, and the more you try to hold on to that old model, the less we're going to listen to you.

Size Doesn't Matter—Relationships Do
••••••••••••••••••••••••••••••••

Institutional authority—an attribute resulting from our belief that organizations and businesses have more expertise on certain subjects than ordinary people—has long been tied to size. The larger the institution, the more credibility it was thought to have—and thus more influence in swaying our decision making. Today, it no longer matters how many sheer numbers we have behind us in the world of social networks; much more critical are the ways in which we are engaging with smaller numbers of people who care about, and take action on, the things we care about.

For mass media, bigger always has meant better. You needed capital to own a printing press, and the more papers you sold, the bigger your empire became. Quantifiable metrics, such as the number of subscribers or viewers, were key, because that's how ad dollars were determined.

If you think about it, though, those numbers were padded in a big way—in terms of television viewership numbers, for example, not every cable subscriber is watching every channel. Even the Nielsen ratings, which seek to pinpoint these numbers for the benefit of advertisers, aren't accurate—they can't accurately determine that every single person watched every minute of that half-hour program on that one channel.

Measuring authority based on sheer numbers is also an imperfect approach when it comes to digital media and social networks. There's no easy way to rank relevance in the online space (yet); the sheer number of friends or followers you have on any given social network service doesn't tell you that much about your authority or influence.

No one can guarantee that each and every one of those people is genuinely invested in the material you're posting. You can't count on people to be committed to any kind of action you ask for, simply because large numbers of people are consuming the material. People are far more likely to be moved by information when it's been shared by someone they trust; the ways in which we measure influence, then, must also change. Less important are sheer numbers, and more important are measurements of relationships, analysis of what makes particular pieces of content more prone to sharing, and how a person's place in the social network ecosystem affects the sharing that does take place. In a blog post that discusses the role of authority, from traditional media to Twitter, Jeff Jarvis, academic and author of *What Would Google Do?* (HarperBusiness, 2009), articulates this phenomenon nicely:

> I think there is no easy measure, but if it exists it will be found instead in relationships: seeing how an idea spreads (because it is relevant and resonates) and what role people have in that (creating the idea, finding it, spreading it, analyzing it) and what one thinks of those people.[7]

If we keep obsessing about social network numbers the way we have over numbers of visitors to our websites, or numbers of subscribers to our newsletters, we're going to fail at being effective when reaching out to the people who might want or need the most to hear the stories we have to share. In fact, sometimes smaller numbers of followers and fans who have been culled and cultivated have a much greater ultimate impact than a large audience you don't know that much about. Michelle Greer, a web marketing strategist, explains the situation deftly using some simple math and Twitter:

1. A person who blogs about foreign films starts following people who tweet about movies like "Dinner with Andre" or are tweeting about the Cannes Film Festival while it is occurring. By tweeting back and forth and engaging people, tweeting unique links, this person gets 2,000 followers. Many of these followers have over 1,000 film obsessed followers themselves.

2. Another person buys followers, follows people just so they follow back, etc. The whole mentality of "I'll follow you only if you follow back" is just childish. Tim O'Reilly offers useful info all the time and will probably never follow me in my lifetime. So what? Anyway, by playing this numbers game, this person gets a whopping 25,000 followers who are more concerned about reciprocal followers than actually getting useful information.

Say I'm marketing a foreign film. If I have these people tweet something with the intention of it getting as much exposure as possible, the person with 2,000 followers will probably be of more use to me. Why? Because this person will get retweeted by people who actually care what I have to say, who would have a lot to offer their own followers by retweeting my stuff. Do the math:

> 2000 people exposed initially
> 50 retweets
> × 6000 unique followers among these retweeters
> 600,000,000 possible impressions

> vs. 25,000 possible impressions for person #2[8]

This mode of outreach turns the traditional concept of an influential communicator on its head. Bigger used to be better, but now, *effective* is better.[9] And there's no easy ranking system for effectiveness; it's so dependent on individual goals that no one can possibly say, "These are the top 10 most effective people in the entire world of social networking."[10]

The shift in how we measure influence also enables us to build authority on the basis of the quality of our ideas, rather than on a stacked deck of influence based on social structures like gender, race, and class. To get into the old-school top 10 lists, we likely had to have a lot of things going for us, including how we looked or where we came from. In the social network sphere, we are the ones determining what and who is relevant and influential to the work we're doing and the lives we're living. When we share our experiences and opinions, we create the opportunities to establish ourselves as authorities in places that were previously the domain of only an elite few. With many more voices, and many more diverse sources of authority and information, we can begin to change how we operate culturally.

Avoiding the Newest Numbers Trap

The growing number of available sources and—in particular—sources that are becoming authoritative on a variety of subjects means that it's getting harder to sift through all the information that's shared and to find people we consider relevant and useful. Traditionally, the sifting and filtering was done for us by institutional authorities, using top-down structured directories that informed us of who the most popular people or organizations were—think of all the magazine and newspaper articles that come out every year listing the top movies, restaurants, books, etc. The dizzying number of participants in social networks make that process much more challenging and much less productive.

We have to fight the urge, however, to simplify our social networking lives by adding ourselves to social media directories that quantify our numbers, rather than qualifying our experiences. In 2009, social networking folks were all abuzz with the launch of several Twitter-related services—such as weFollow, Twittorati, and a few others—that rank Twitter users according to their "popularity," which is defined by the person's number of followers or popularity in the blogosphere.

So-called popularity does not make these folks automatically interesting or relevant.

Using these directories and recommending relationships based on the number of followers can be confusing and misleading. When you're just getting started, it's easy to fall into the trap of, "Oh, I should follow celebrity-name-here because a million other people do, so that person must be interesting." Afraid not.

Moreover, following and friending based on pure numbers also reinforces traditional hierarchies that historically have kept diverse voices out of mainstream conversations. Numbers hide the mostly invisible, marginalizing social structures that we discussed in chapter 2. When we follow people blindly based on how popular we perceive them to be or how popular the culture perceives them to be, we're excluding the depth of content from numerous other sources on the edges (versus the cool kids in the center, or top), who are often more relevant, interesting, and worth sharing.

A much more effective strategy for establishing your authority is to choose a few people you know and look at who they're communicating with. Study those people's profiles and what they've written recently, and see if they intrigue you or if you have something in common. You'll find some specific tips on how to do this in the resource guides at the end of the book.

Someday, maybe even while this book is being printed, my dream of having an application that shows me "interestingness"

How "interestingness" might work.

in the social network sphere will come true. Flickr has this for photographs: There is an algorithm based on "[w]here the click-throughs are coming from; who comments on it and when; who marks it as a favorite; its tags and many more things which are constantly changing."[11] The best part? Interestingness itself, then, is constantly changing, based on these shifting variables, so there's a good chance of finding both something new and something surprising when one goes spelunking through Flickr's massive collection of interesting photos.

I'm not going to lie to you: This great shift in authority isn't the easiest part of social networking's brave new world to navigate. The tools give us tremendous power to change the culture around us, but they're new, and our behavior and impressions are still based on operating within a hyper-capitalist-focused, hierarchical mindset. We have a lot of work to do on freeing our minds before the rest of our bits will follow.

Surprisingly, though, the uncertainty of the future of social networking tools is also the good news: *Things are still shaking out*, and we're in a position to determine whether the reordering of authority will benefit people who previously did not have the access or the means to make their voices heard. Armed with a fundamental understanding of what's taking place (by, ahem, reading good books on the subject), you're primed to make the most of change.[12]

An Abundance of Attention
• •

Just as we need to develop new skills to think about the volume of information we're receiving, so too do we need new skills for managing our attention span. Because of the market structure of mass communications, we often think of our attention in terms of economics; in recent years, there's been lots of talk in media and technology circles about the *attention economy*. If you're new to the term, here's the basic idea: Attention is scarce, meaning it's a finite commodity that can be gathered and exhausted. Using economics as a model, we have to choose where we "spend" our attention, and those seeking to gain our attention have to use market-based tactics—aka "marketing"! aha!—to win the privilege of our spending our attention on them.

As we enter a more social, and perhaps more holistic, way of interacting with the world around us, squeezing our attention span in this kind of transaction-based, market model is turning out to be fraught with problems. Our attention span, as it turns out, is not in the limited supply that marketers would have us believe.

Market models and economies are attractive to us as a culture because we're so familiar with transaction-based economies. As discussed in chapter 3, it's hard for us to think about commodities in any other way, because we're so focused on a tit-for-tat system as a measuring stick for fairness in labor, time, and services.

When we apply transactions to how traditional media work (think: one-directional, few-to-many broadcast messages), it's easy to see how we ended up with today's dismal state of affairs: reality TV, infotainment news, etc. If, as a producer of content in a market-based system, I need to get the most bang for my buck out of each "transaction," I'm going to create something that will gain the most attention. I'll have to yell the loudest, create the most spectacle. It's not worth my time or money to create niche content that will draw in specific kinds of audiences; partly because this is one-directional and I have all the control, I can blast people with content and hope for the best out of that transactional moment, when I print an article or air a show. The more outrageous that content is, the better chance I have of at least catching people's eye for a moment—take advantage of humanity's rubbernecking instinct.

How the transactional moment works is changing rapidly, thanks to social networks. First, the moment is more bidirectional (or even multidirectional) than ever. We're having conversations with one another, so the transaction is not just about my producing content and your consuming it. It's about how we interact with what gets put out there and how that content changes once we start interacting with it.

This moment in social and technological development is also different because it's not a few-to-many model; it's a many-to-many model. Applying an economic analysis to attention now becomes messy.

We have to reframe our interactions with one another—we shouldn't be thinking about trying to "pay attention" to everything that comes our way and then running out of attention to pay. We need to make the world around us a stream or flow of information, and dip in and out of that flow as necessary or desired. Attention, in this model, isn't a scarce commodity; it's an unending stream that weaves in and out of other streams. (Suddenly I'm having a *Ghostbusters* moment.) As web visionary Stowe Boyd argues,

> The answer is not becoming obsessed with attention as a limited resource to be husbanded, or thinking of our cognition as a laser beam to be pointed at only at what is important.
>
> We need to unfocus, to rely more on the network or tribe to surface things of importance, and remain open to new opportunities: these are potentially more important than the work on the desk. Don't sharpen the knife too much.[13]

Since attention isn't composed of chunks that accumulate and are doled out in this way of thinking, it's fairly useless to consider the system a finite economy. Those who yell the loudest and make the biggest fools of themselves will become less important as our notions of celebrity also change—having higher numbers of viewers or followers or fans doesn't equal influence and fame. Or, at least it doesn't have to. If we can turn around our thinking, away from the style of mass media that has only served to alienate us from one another and has produced lowest-common-denominator content, and toward a more holistic, ecosystem-like view in which relationships to and relevancy of content matter, then attention's scarcity also begins to disappear.

Once scarcity is removed from the model, market economics doesn't apply to it. You're not competing for others' attention; you're creating sustainable relationships across which content flows, many ways. What happens as a result of those relationships might be quantifiable in some way, but how we choose to measure them absolutely must become more nuanced than units of product sold, page views/uniques, or number of followers/fans gained. This is another key point missing from many of the conversations about social media's impact: We are at a critical cultural juncture where it is up to us to experiment and ultimately define how things work in the ecosystem.

Information Wildfires
• • • • • • • • • • • • • • • • •

As social networks shift our perceptions of authority, we also have to guard against the pitfalls that can happen when large numbers of people have access to information without the context that they're used to. Institutional authorities provided this context in the past; now that organic authority plays more of a role in how we receive information and how quickly we receive it, we have a new responsibility to ensure the accuracy of reporting of external events that we share.

Social networks can spread information like wildfire. Marketers know this, and some spend oodles of time and money trying to figure out how to make something "go viral."

News, on the other hand, doesn't need a marketing genius. Regardless of whether the subject is celebrity gossip or the latest economic statistics, news headlines can reach viral proportions that would make any marketer proud. Never before have so many people had instantaneous access to so much unfiltered information. We're quick to act on that information—and to share it with everyone we know.

While sharing news is generally a good thing (hey, you're reading *Share This!*), we're not necessarily equipped to process and react responsibly when we're hit with surprising or salacious news—or information that provokes a strong emotional response. We tend to share first and ask questions later, and, as we'll see below, doing so can cause serious damage and distrust.

Part of this shortcoming is biological: The section of our brain that reacts to emotional content, the amygdala, isn't the most sophisticated piece of machinery. It interprets and paints events and emotions in broad strokes, most simply as positive or negative. Not a lot of nuance there.

The rest of our brain is supposed to help by engaging and filtering information based on context. We're supposed to take into account physical actions, such as a person's body language and the tone of conversation, as well as our surroundings. Digital media doesn't provide these cues, so the other parts of our brain aren't activated. In fact, research shows that e-mail flaming (inappropriate negative reactions expressed publicly online) is a result of these missing cues.[14]

It could be said, then, that without adequate understanding and even training around using social networks during times of crisis, we're doomed to a mob mentality. Holding back the mob can be the challenging side of sharing our stories; we'll talk later in this section about how to apply some common media literacy skills to our own networks.

I'm Not Dead Yet: Stopping Info Misflow
• •

It used to be that we heard about major news events from sources with institutional authority—a news company with investigative journalists and fact checkers, for instance. Think of breaking-news moments that we associate with well-known and highly respected authority figures: Walter Cronkite removing his glasses and announcing the death of President Kennedy, or Tom Brokaw broadcasting the fall of the Berlin Wall.

Now we collectively experience events in real time, and everyone is a potential newscaster. Our culture, with its recent hyperfocus on breaking news,[15] hasn't prepared us to deal with the impact of what we share with one another during those events and how we handle the information that bombards us. New media tools and social networks have given us new ways to spread information—and new questions to ask about our responsibility.

The events of June 25, 2009, provide an excellent illustration of how misinformation centered around breaking news can spread quickly across social networks. Both Michael Jackson and Farrah Fawcett died that day. Across many social networks, people expressed their surprise and grief at the loss of two pop-culture icons. Then came news on the same social networks that actor Jeff Goldblum had also died, on a movie set in New Zealand. A quick Google search turned up a hit for a news story on MoviesOnline.com, reporting the death.[16] Many people began sharing the news (yours truly included). Tapping into cultural superstitions about deaths occurring in threes is an especially poignant way to make information go viral, apparently.

Alas, the much-beloved Mr. Goldblum was not dead. He wasn't even in New Zealand at the time[17]—but the runaway nature of the story allowed it to charge into the social network sphere and stay there for a good 24 hours, even after it was officially debunked within an hour or two of its first mention (via an institutional authority: Goldblum's agent).[18] In a case like this, 24 hours of presuming a popular actor's death isn't likely to do any serious damage (except, perhaps, to the actor's ego), but when the news is more critical, 24 hours is plenty of time to inflame passions and cause people to act, sometimes unwisely, on misinformation.

Before the Internet, we assessed the authority of our peers and relied on them to share trustworthy information, with some degree of success (and failure—I grew up thinking I'd die if I simultaneously ate Pop Rocks and drank a Coke[19]). The Internet hits the scene, and suddenly there's an explosion of urban legends. Remember those e-mail chains where a little boy with cancer only wished to see his e-mail forwarded around?

Urban legends and hoaxes make emotional appeals that force us to address our common cultural fears (death, terror, freaky candy that pops in your mouth). If we trust the information source (often a friend or family member), we usually believe the information is true—we transfer a person's general trustworthiness to individual bits of news without verifying whether the information is correct.

But if someone repeatedly shares enough false information, we naturally respond by lowering the authority that person has in the news-sharing department. Quick survey: How many people don't read e-mails from Aunt Beatrice anymore because she sent the human organ theft hoax again?

We're at roughly the same level with social networks right now as we were with e-mail in the late 1990s and early 2000s. The tools are new and snazzy, and we don't yet have a sophisticated understanding of the role they play in our lives.

And it's not just we or our family members who have become enamored with these new tools. Look at the mainstream media's coverage of breaking news today. News anchors actually read tweets and Facebook posts on air as a method of sharing news. That's not just silly; it's also irresponsible.

When Twittering Goes Awry
••••••••••••••••••••••

The Iranian election protests of 2009 provided a more serious teachable moment concerning authority and information dissemination. The background: In June 2009, Iran held a presidential election in which the incumbent, Mahmoud Ahmadinejad, claimed to win 62% of the vote.[20] Challenger Mir-Hossein Mousavi, a marginally reformist candidate who supports more freedom and democracy in Iran, publicly questioned the results and asked his supporters to protest nonviolently.[21]

Protesters took to the streets on June 13, 2009, and the country's sophisticated community of political (and personal) bloggers started sharing news about public assemblies—and subsequent police crackdowns. A few people posted first-person accounts on blogs and on social networks like Facebook and Twitter, as well as via SMS texting on mobile phones (before the government shut down the cell phone networks). People outside of the country picked up what was happening and shared it with their networks. News spread rapidly, especially as the police violence escalated.

In the United States, news junkies and politicos marveled at the fact that the major cable news outlets—CNN, MSNBC, Fox News—weren't covering the election. Viewers started pressuring the networks to get on the story. On Twitter, a hashtag (a keyword to indicate what topic the tweet is covering) was created to convey unhappiness about the missing coverage, targeting CNN in particular: #CNNfail.[22]

It seemed the pressure worked. By the following morning, CNN and other news networks were broadcasting information about the events as they unfolded. Where they tripped up was when they started calling the events in Iran the first "Twitter revolution" and started relying heavily on social networks as sources. Ditching the familiar resources that give news outlets institutional authority—such as trained journalists and analysts familiar with Iranian politics—journalists instead jumped on a hot, trendy bandwagon. Without verifying the accuracy of many of the reports, mainstream news organizations broadcast a host of misinformation about the events inside Iran, including how many people were protesting, who was firing on the crowds, and how many people had died.

Everyday people on social networks were susceptible to the same bandwagon mentality. The high emotional content of the information coming out of Iran drove people to share first and source later. The resulting confusion of reports being shared outside of Iran didn't necessarily lead directly to the arrests or deaths of protesters, but the proliferation of misinformation did create a mythology about the impact that social networking tools had on life-changing events inside a repressive regime. To a large extent, Iranian protesters were not using Twitter, and the cell phone network had been shut down. By perpetuating the myth that protesters were subverting a dangerous, repressive, totalitarian regime purely with shiny new technology, mainstream media and participants who shared misinformation created a dangerous situation for the next conflict, in which dissenters could mistakenly believe that these tools alone would save their lives.[23] Technology of any kind, especially in countries run by despots, will not absolve us from responsibility for the difficult, and dangerous, work of organizing against power structures that threaten lives.

Lessons of Iran's Aftermath

As the hierarchy of news and authority changes, we have to dismantle the "winner takes all" mentality of breaking news. There's always a rush to be the first person or organization with the news, because being first is a near-surefire way to increase traffic, and more traffic often means more ad dollars. But as we learned previously, the model of information distribution that's reliant on sheer numbers is changing rapidly, and when pursued single-mindedly, this strategy will ultimately fail (thank goodness).

As consumers, we have to help ensure that other factors—such as validity and relevancy—are taken into account. Professional journalists and media organizations also need to practice sustainability through the emerging "slow news"[24] movement—a recommitment to investigation and validation of information that is not dependent on the 24-hour news cycle.

Already, blogs and other independent news organizations are seeing the benefits of producing thoughtful analysis and content that ultimately garners high traffic. Our Bodies Our

Blog, the blog for the *Our Bodies, Ourselves* (Touchstone, 2005) women's health book, published an informative analysis on the new government mammogram guidelines in 2009, one day after the guidelines were released.[25] There was much hype and anger but little straightforward information floating around in the first 24 hours, and the post hit home for many. It was passed around extensively on social networks and linked to from a variety of popular blogs, like Daily Kos. "There was a thirst for thoughtful analysis," said Christine Cupaiuolo, the post's author and coeditor of the blog. "We weren't the first ones out of the gate with a response, but we provided what people were looking for—perspective and research."

We have to demand more accountability from our sources, regardless of who they might be. We may not have the benefit of the physical cues (voice and body language), but we have learned over time to be more savvy news consumers. And we've come to demand accountability—whether we get our news from large, well-funded companies or from small blogs. We need to apply skepticism and critical thinking skills to our networks as well. Finally, we have to learn a new kind of media literacy, one where we are not simply reacting. I'm reminded of the advice we were given as kids: If you're on fire, "stop, drop, and roll." Try this: If your news stream is on fire, stop, drop, and *think*. Take a moment to process the information you receive and verify it through authoritative sources.

It's important that we choose wisely. As we've discussed before, all of us have a critical role to play in the changing nature of authority and in determining who becomes valued as a trusted news source. As we create new guidelines for coming generations, we have a responsibility to support spaces where diverse voices are heard, varied experiences are shared, and trustworthy information is spread.

Your Networks Save the Day
••••••••••••••••••••••••

The trickiness of a world in which authority is up for grabs means that understanding and navigating organic authority is challenging. And having numerous sources sharing information with us means it can be tough to build organic authority in the cacophony. Now that anyone can publish anything, and all this technology has created maps and pathways for easy communication across our social networks, an amazing amount of information is hurtling toward us (duck!).

Because we've not yet figured out how to harness different aspects of these new technologies, we're at a point of social technology where many, many influences are converging on us. And one of the biggest challenges we face is the beast of the digital age: information overload. Not managing your information can be the difference between making a difference in the world and giving up altogether.

The good news is that your relationships will save your sanity as the onslaught of information comes at you. Certainly the technologies will advance and change to deal with overload, but we're collectively experiencing a shift in the culture where we trust and rely on one another to filter, curate, and point out the critical information. Returning to the DNA theory, where similarity of ideas and voices breeds staleness and limited progress, the fact that we have so many voices to choose from now works to our advantage: We have a fresh mix—ever more interesting as new people come on board—to work with when we're all in there sharing our stories.

There are a couple of ways to approach the new TMI: (1) reframe what's happening so that we all understand that we don't have to deal with everything that comes at us,[26] and (2) get savvy on tools and tips that will help us manage our digital clutter. My approach is blended; in this section, we'll do the reframing, and later in resource guides, we'll go over some tips for managing information flow. The key is to understand that authority is the basis by which we can use our relationships to accomplish this.

One of the questions I get asked most about social networks is, "OK, I understand how it technically works now, but how do you handle that flood of information coming your way? It would drive me crazy to try to keep track of *x* number of people!"

Here's the secret: You're not "keeping track" of people on social networks. If I tried to read every message from the hundreds of people I follow in all the conversations on the social networks I participate in, I would (a) never get any work done, (b) go slightly bonkers, and thus (c) be rendered homeless quite quickly. The trick is to not pay *precise* attention to all those people all the time.

The culture of e-mail, our main form of digital communication for the past 10-plus years, creates the expectation that every message on our screens is important enough to demand our attention. We are asked to evaluate sometimes hundreds of messages a day: Do I ignore, delete, reply, archive, or forward? As the popularity of e-mail has grown, we've become more frustrated and overwhelmed.

Now, with social networks, we are connected to even more people, more of the time. The great shift in authority, spurred by new technologies, gives unprecedented numbers of people and organizations the ability to push information our way. But the tools and our culture are not yet in sync. We're being flooded, and we're not sure what to do with it all.

Prior to this giant shift, we relied on others to be the dams and gatekeepers—we didn't really have a choice. Newspaper editors decided which stories were important enough to publish, advertisers told us which products were good to buy, advocacy organizations showed us where help was needed, politicians told us . . . something.

Now the dam is open. What do we do? We're trained to look at each message and act on it (or file it until we're guilt-ridden for *not* acting on it). If we're disconnected from technology for any period of time, we're taught to go back and catch up on what we missed. As the information flow increases, we feel like we're spending more time catching up, and less time connecting and acting.

One problem with e-mail is that it's fundamentally the same tool it started out as back in the 1970s. The technology of e-mail hasn't evolved to help us manage serious amounts of information coming our way, and while we have folders and filters to shuffle messages around with,[27] we're still completely at the mercy of everyone who has our e-mail address. What's worse, a good chunk of those people who send us things expect some sort of response. It's no wonder that people take drastic measures, like declaring "e-mail bankruptcy."[28]

The differences between e-mail and social networks are vast, and understanding the dissimilarities can prepare us to be more effective with our communication as we organize for change. We'll go into some of the nitty-gritty tactics in the resource guides, but these key concepts should help you get started: First, when we choose to participate on social networks, we actively choose whom we share with and whom we want to hear from. On social networks like Twitter, where that choice doesn't have to be reciprocal, we have a good deal of freedom to be very specific about whose sharing we want to read. Second, people sharing on social networks don't expect a response to what they share. It's a bonus if someone replies or comments, but not many people walk around thinking that all of their friends or followers have read everything they've shared.[29] Third, social networking software, while still very much in its infancy, is designed to make sense of the flow of information. Some features of various networks may replicate the dastardly conundrums of e-mail, but overall the movement in social software design is away from individual message interactions and toward an overview of your personal network ecosystem.

Your Networks' Role in Building and Managing Your Authority—Sanely

This mantra will change your life and help you on your way to using these tools to change the world: You don't have to pay attention to everything. Think of the flow of information that's coming your way as a river—created from trusted, authoritative sources you've established—that you occasionally dip into to see what's happening. When you're not at the river, there's no way to know what's going by. And here's the kicker, folks: You have to learn to be Okay With That.

The big secret of all those people you see with thousands of friends and followers in social networks? They're fine with the fact that they are going to miss things, sometimes lots of things. They don't let any one authority—institutional or organic—run their lives. Take a deep breath, say a few *oms* if that's your thing, and move along.

Remember that those big numbers do not necessarily equal influence *or* authority. Rather than focusing on the broadcast model of "Bigger is better," it's more important for you, in your personal information management system, to be selective in what you choose to take in. Less is often more in social media.

Ditching the broadcast model also means relying on your network—as well as some nifty tools we'll discuss later—to get you the really important stuff. Remember that game you played at camp, when you'd fall backward and have faith that your campmates were going to catch you? It's kind of like that, only without the stomach-dropping-inducing nausea. You're going to learn, over time, that you can trust your network to provide what you need. You'll learn to ask for help and more information—and if you're practicing the good social capitalist karma that we discussed in chapter 3, you'll get it. Let's say you're interested in news and conversations on green jobs. You go into meetings that last all day, and when you return, you decide to browse through your social networks to see if anything happened. Rather than pore over every message that was posted since you last checked, you'll instead glance through recent messages and see what's been shared and reshared by your green jobs people, and you'll quickly scan alerts and filters that you've set up (because you've read how to do so in the resource guides) to make sure that important bits squeeze through. It's not a matter of digging into every last message; it's more learning how to effectively browse for relevant information from a big-picture point of view.

Thus, the task at hand for each of us is twofold:

- Be choosy and intentioned about where your information is coming from. Realize that it's up to you to find experts who are relevant to your life, and to explore unfamiliar territory in the search for new authorities. Include race, gender, class, and sexuality as factors to consider. Make your connections a mix of people you know and don't know.

- Make sure you're adding *your* voice to the conversations. So much of what we know or think is true about how information spreads, and how that relates to social change, is in flux right now. All of us have to be willing to take part in this exciting experiment.

Playing by New Rules
• • • • • • • • • • • • • • • •

Armed with the power to subvert traditional power structures by establishing our own authority, as well as having the ability to assign authority to others, we are being released from the hierarchical dependencies that have kept our stories from reaching one another on a massive scale. We can change whom and what we consider influential in our culture, and as long as we develop the skills we need to act responsibly in the face of a flood of new information, we can tackle the societal structures that constrain us.

The free-for-all nature of this shift in authority offers opportunities for progress, but deep and lasting change won't emerge unless we also recognize the biases we bring to the table, as well as the fears that might be holding us back.

5 Sharing Is Daring

THE EASE WITH which we share information—responsibly and thoughtfully, of course—enables us to move on social justice issues at speeds that were previously unimaginable. That speed, combined with the bias that each of us brings to the table, and our own fears and hesitancy, can come with traps—both perceived and real. Maneuvering around old-style thinking that can keep us out of conversations that desperately need us—and can unintentionally marginalize others—is critical to ensuring that we connect with one another in ways that will support changing the world.

Free-for-All Organizing, and the Secret Tyrants We All Are

One weekend in April 2009, Amazon.com removed 58,000 books from its sales ranking system, effectively removing these books from the website. Most contained feminist, LGBT, and sex-positive content; they mysteriously received an "adult" flag while heteronormative sexual products, like Playboy calendars and antigay screeds, remained untouched.

Murmurs began on Twitter. Authors were confused when their books could no longer be found, and consumers started posting about failed searches. Through the use of a hashtag (in this case, #AmazonFAIL), participants were able to track all of the related posts about Amazon. Within a few hours, enough information had been gathered to show the types of books that were being flagged.

"Have fun stormin' the castle!" (Miracle Max in *The Princess Bride*)

The flames were fanned higher, and soon various "web celebrities" took up the cause, using their social capital and influence to share stories about books that were being, in effect, digitally banned. Not long after, several newspapers caught wind of the firestorm—the *Los Angeles Times* blogged the de-ranking that Sunday evening—Easter Sunday, as it happened.[1] By later that night, Amazon couldn't help but make a statement in response. A spokesperson told *Publishers Weekly*[2] that the de-ranking problem was a "glitch" and that Amazon was looking into it.[3]

Now, imagine the same scenario just 10 years ago. Amazon, even then, was a popular online retailer with a good amount of credibility. If a huge swath of books had been removed from the site in 1999, how would people have protested? It would have been through angry e-mails to the corporate offices. Op-eds might have been pitched to various newspapers, and over several days and weeks, various civil rights groups might have gotten involved. In short, everyday people would have had to rely on a slow-moving hierarchical system with lots of gatekeepers along the way deciding if this was a worthwhile issue.

Instead, in 2009, these voices slipped into the consciousness of the web, created a campaign without any organization or funding, and forced Amazon to respond within 24 hours. And to ice that cake, the mainstream media played catch-up in the following days, scrambling for scraps of the story.

Score a big one for social networks!

Before we think that this success story proves we've mastered the art of instant, free-for-all organizing, let's remember that we've been down a somewhat similar road before, and we learned some lessons that can carry over to social networks and social media. Endeavors organized on the fly, without constraints or guidelines that organizations bring—like the Amazon uproar, in which no advocacy group orchestrated any of the actions that were taken—often ignore or silence voices that must be part of the conversations and movements we're creating.

Remember chapter 3's discussion of consciousness-raising in the women's movement of the late 1960s and early 1970s? Though women's groups often illuminated a path toward activism and organizing, these groups also marginalized the voices and experiences of women of color and queer women.

Let me give you a brief rundown of what happened: Feminists decided that the societal structures in place were largely restrictive and oppressive to women. Therefore, the best way to break free was to organize without formal hierarchies and leaders, which were considered the source of the oppression.

Funny thing: When you remove *explicit* structure from a group—leaders, hierarchies, process—it turns out that *implicit* structure arises. What do I mean by implicit? Well, people's personal biases, for starters. Sticking with our historical study, many of these groups organized around the concerns of mainly white, middle-class, straight women, choosing (either consciously or unconsciously) not to include other voices.

When implicit structure takes over—for example, the idea that we are all equal on the Internet and it's completely up-by-our-bootstraps—we run the risk of entering a series of vicious cycles that prevent fundamental, systemic change from emerging. By pretending that these implicit biases don't exist or don't matter, we ignore the voices of those most affected by the issues we care about, and we reinforce the very power structures that we seek to break down. In a critical 1970 paper, feminist scholar and author Jo Freeman labeled this phenomenon of marginalizing minority-represented voices "the tyranny of structurelessness":

> This means that to strive for a "structureless" group is as useful, and as deceptive, as to aim at an "objective" news story, "value-free" social science or a "free" economy. A "laissez-faire" group is about as realistic as a "laissez-faire" society; the idea becomes a smokescreen for the strong or the lucky to establish unquestioned hegemony over others. . . . Thus "structurelessness" becomes a way of masking power.[4]

Because of the social stratification that currently exists online, as discussed in chapter 2, we are seeing the repercussions of digital structurelessness manifest in many ways. Our tendency to congregate around like-minded folk is understandable and very human, but it can be dangerous when organizing around issues for change. I'm not advocating reaching out to opposing viewpoints at every juncture; I'm recommending making sure that a number of diverse perspectives are in the echo chambers we're creating.[5] In many cases, we need to look hard at who is most affected by the issues we're working on and ensure that they're being heard.

People with any kind of privilege—social, economic, even technological—tend to believe that the work they are doing on behalf of those with less privilege is helpful, because they know better. Thinking you know better doesn't win change, it wins you an ego trip. In fall 2009, the U.S. House of Representatives passed a health care reform bill that included an amendment, sponsored by conservative Democrat Bart Stupak, containing the most restrictive legislation on reproductive rights in over 40 years. On social networks, women expressed their outrage at having been "thrown under the bus" in favor of pushing through the reform. Some men were sympathetic to the pain that women were expressing, but many sought to explain why the amendment was passed, how they were sure it wouldn't pass the Senate, and other legislative nuances of the situation. Instead of expressing empathetic outrage, they chose to teach women what they felt must not be clear about the situation— which only intensified women's alienation from the process, and their overall shock and disillusionment. Engaging with, listening to, and *hearing* people who have different backgrounds from yours starts a fundamental process for change, and social networks hold a lot of promise for making the networks we belong to more diverse.

How do we engage with diverse groups of people in online public spaces? The power law tells us that those with the largest audiences will continue to build their audiences exponentially.[6] The sneak attack, though, is that we're not talking *just* about audience size; we're talking about multiple conversations, and effective ones at that. In order to have those effective conversations, though, we have to chart a course of action to acknowledge our biases, so then we can start reaching out and connecting with people who don't share our same points of reference.

To be clear, we won't ever *eliminate* our biases. But we can begin to be explicit about what we learn about ourselves and our social spheres when bias rears its ugly head. Social technology researcher danah boyd suggests a series of questions for that explicit discovery process: "*None* of us is going to be unbiased. There is no way to be unbiased. The question is: Can you account for your biases? Can you recognize when they get in the way? Can you open up a dialogue, even if it makes you uncomfortable, with people who aren't like you?"[7] Opening ourselves up to that process and beginning to break out of the way we've been thinking about how we assume the world operates (simply because it's operated like that for a long time) is crucial. We need to listen as selflessly as possible to what others are sharing and make sure that we're not perpetuating restrictive social structures. It's important to start by recognizing what it feels like when you've been triggered to react, as many people who practice meditation do. For me, I can feel my chest tighten and my ears burn, as if I've been deeply wronged in some way. Before I react outwardly to that feeling, I try to step outside of it and observe it. Then I always seem to remember something my mom asked us when we were kids and were caught making fun of or picking on someone else: "How would you feel if that were you?" It makes me realize that often those moments are not about *me* at all—they are about larger injustices that I have a role in changing or stopping altogether, and it's my job to figure out how to do that.

Addressing one's biases is a deeply uncomfortable process. There, I've said it. It's hard, and it requires a lot of psychological work that nobody wants to deal with. Because really, no one wants to feel like or be called a bigot, right? Or at least, most *sane* people don't want to.

How to Be a Useful Agent of Change
••••••••••••••••••••••••••••••

None of us are off the hook here, folks—regardless of whether you're a liberal blogger writing tirelessly about health care reform, a person of color working for racial justice in media, a feminist advocating for reproductive freedom, or a queer activist lobbying for marriage rights. Yes, you get good karma for doing that work, and you're a better person for it (that's your gold star for today!). But none of us are above anyone else in this big-picture struggle. Don't assume that your status in one arena you are passionate about somehow makes you invulnerable to having privilege, and bias, in others. You've got to take your blinders off if we're going to have half a chance with this.

The first step is to recognize that we have a problem. Say this out loud: "Hi, my name is _____ and I have many biases."

Step two: *Listen* to the people around you. The best defense is not a good offense; it's checking your ego and listening to what others are saying without assuming you're in the right.

Meeting people where they are is critical to the process. You can't force anyone to see your point of view, but making the effort to engage from a common-ground starting point can make all the difference in the world. Social media consultant and political blogger Cheryl Contee, partner and cofounder of Fission Strategy, points to President Barack Obama's background bridging experiences while growing up in both black and white worlds as an example of finding common ground in action. "He had to learn to seamlessly create relationships with different kinds of people," says Contee. "That skill is necessary online."[8] Our goodwill and intentions are not enough; in the work of ambassadorship, we have to recognize that other people's perceptions of us are valid based on their own experiences. When we meet people there, the sharing we do has a greater chance of building bonds between allies.[9]

Step three: Remember that eliminating oppression is *good for everybody*. As W. F. Hightower, the father of my favorite populist pundit, Jim Hightower, likes to say, "Everyone does better when everyone does better."[10] Diversity is a strategic imperative for achieving collective goals. As diversity scholar Roosevelt Thomas notes, we all make better decisions—as individuals and as a society—when we account for differences and tensions.[11]

Social media and social networks provide us with the tools to accomplish a whole lot. Once you've completed your three-step process, it's time to sign yourself up as an ambassador to a social sphere that has nothing to do with your identity or what privilege you bring to the table. It'll be very *Stranger in a Strange Land* for you, trust me. If you're white, find people of color to follow on Twitter. Straight? Look at fan pages and groups of different LGBTQQI groups on Facebook.

It's important for people of all stripes and places to engage with those who are different from themselves, but to be blunt, it's extra important for those who are a couple of notches up on the hierarchy to go through this exercise. Remember, you're not there as part of some sociology experiment, but because you get that progress is possible only when we participate. (Check out the resource guides for finding new people on social networks.)

A crucial part of cross-pollination exercises is realizing that your role as ambassador is *not* to defend your position in the food chain. That's where a lot of us get into trouble—I know I have. Your job is to recognize what privilege you bring—whether it's your gender, your class, your race, your sexuality, etc.—and figure out how best you can use it to enable justice for people who don't share your privilege. Jessica Hoffman, editor of *make/ shift* magazine, pithily captured our collective responsibility to engage in self-reflection in an article she wrote about a white feminist's role in other social justice movements: "Inexperienced because of privilege, we hadn't thought well on our feet, and we'd been in a certain denial about how bad things might get; *we'd been pissed and well meaning, but not useful* [emphasis mine]."[12] It's the job of all of us to be useful.

This is the work, folks! The challenges are numerous. But without an honest look at structural divides, we can't break them down. You'll be digging deep as you go in, but you won't be alone. Being together in this endeavor is the first part of tackling the challenges. The second is addressing—and overcoming—the fears that keep us out of the conversations that are happening on social networks.

Lions and Tigers and Bears! Oh, My(Space)! The Fears People Have
• • • • • • • • • • • • • • • • •

Fear of the unknown can add to the social divisions lurking in social technology. By far the most common complaint I hear from all different kinds of people is that their lack of knowledge about how something works causes them to distrust the benefits they might gain from it. The various waves of hype around children's safety in social networks and when using cell phones, for example, are largely a result of parents' lack of education about how the technologies function, and how they might work with the technologies within their families. Mainstream media's number-one-selling product is fear, so they capitalize on parents' fear of the unknown to sell their stories. Since the 1990s, the availability of porn on the Internet has been used as a scare tactic for news stories and legislation calling for the widespread restriction of access to the new technologies.[13] If we had a better understanding of how technologies work, we would all be better equipped to address the role they play in our lives. But when fear of technology makes us hesitate, or holds us back altogether, the conversations about social change continue on without us—without the benefit of our experiences, values, and knowledge.

Those who are reluctant to use social networks to effect change also frequently express fear over lost privacy. The challenges we face in maintaining some semblance of privacy while participating in the larger social movement can certainly seem overwhelming. We're communicating more frequently and more openly with people with whom we may not yet have forged alliances in our own spheres. Talking to strangers—what you've been told you're not supposed to do since you were a child—may also make us feel vulnerable as we share who we are as part of the work of change. Rinku Sen, executive director of the Applied Research Center and coauthor of *The Accidental American: Immigration and Citizenship in the Age of Globalization* (Berrett-Koehler Publishers, 2008), points out that these risks are similar to the risks that people working in social justice movements have always experienced; only the scale and intimacy have changed. "That need to address our fears and protect ourselves is a part of doing politics," Sen argues. "The medium is different, and you can hear from strangers more often, but the fear itself is not different. It's legitimate in both places."[14] While the fear feels different because it's related to new technology and experienced in a way that we're not used to, it's the same fear that proponents of social change have always had to confront.

When choosing to do work that's changing the world, even if it's only contributing your life experiences and values to public conversations (which can be risky for some people), examine your network and ask the people in it to support you in the scarier moments. Sen urges potential organizers to have a frank conversation with their community—and themselves—about what level of risk they're willing to take. "It's better to take a risk when you have a lot of people around you watching what's happening than if you're by yourself," she advises.

Other activists have found ways to balance caution and sharing as well. DREAMActivist.org, for example, enables students using social technologies to share stories of undocumented young people who face possible deportation despite the fact that they've grown up in the United States. These students recognize the political danger associated with online activism, but it doesn't stop them from using social media to help folks understand complicated legislation. On Twitter, their postings have become a rich resource of news related to immigration issues.

Let's be clear: Most of us don't have to worry about severe political consequences of speaking out online. But each of us has our own valid concerns that need to be addressed. Every new technology shift inspires anxiety about how our lives will change.

Privacy fears are common; so are fears of reprisal. Will you encounter people who are rude or who seem determined to disagree with whatever you write?[15] Maybe. Should this stop you? Absolutely not.

Remember that social networks generally provide a safe space in which to share our experiences. More often than not, sharing creates empathy, and through that empathy, each connection we make becomes part of a network of allies to call on when things aren't so pretty.

The Monsters Under the Bed

Women, more than men, struggle with the effects of sharing. But before we get there, let's talk a bit about what holds women back from participating in the first place. Some women still believe that the Internet is a dangerous place and people will come get us if we tell them who we are, what we think, and what we're doing. While this attitude is changing as social networks evolve and more people of all ages join in, the fear still holds some women back. All of us—men and women—need to take basic precautions. But warning women away from something "for their own good" has long minimized their participation in the culture.

When women don't participate as fully as men, social justice pays the price. One of the most striking examples of the participation divide is Wikipedia. Almost all of you, I'm assuming, have read something on Wikipedia. But do you know what the typical person who has edited something on Wikipedia looks like? There's a *more than 80% chance that the editor is male.* This means that women are not taking advantage of the opportunity to define and document history.

Even a woman like me, who's fairly freewheelin' about what she'll tell people, needed this information to wake up to the fact that women's participation matters. Up until 2007, I used pseudonyms for screen names; I preapproved everyone who wanted to read my posts on Twitter; and I kept most of my information on other social networks private, at least to some degree. My epiphany came during a Women Who Tech workshop in 2007, when author and speaker Tara Hunt explained that even though I was sharing my experience with a select group of people, I wasn't shaping the *public* conversation.[16] My voice wasn't represented in conversations on changing things that needed to be changed.

Many people have a "lightbulb moment" once they conquer their hesitation or resistance: They find that they have an entirely new landscape of possibilities open to them. Barbara Glickstein, a broadcast journalist who covers public health issues, views her first venture onto Facebook as a transformational experience. "It felt like I had crossed a boundary, which I realized I created in my mind," she said. "Since getting involved in on social networks, the people there have provided me with radio show ideas, guests for my show, insights into progressive causes, and information I would otherwise not have had access to."[17] Once we get over our hesitation and the door to social networks opens, we're offered the tools we need to make change.

Let's look at some of the other fears that people have and figure out a way to manage them.

I don't want people to know about my private life.

That's actually 100% fine. A pervasive myth about social media is that its only purpose is revelatory; we use it to celebrate all our dirty laundry and naughty bits. While I'm personally not averse to the dirty and the naughty, that's far from the whole story and not the reason we're participating on social networks.

In chapter 3, we discussed authenticity: Nothing requires you to share your deepest, darkest secrets. The point of sharing who you are is not to aspire to reality-TV levels of exposure. It's to immerse yourself—or a part of yourself that you feel comfortable sharing—in a conversation that's important and relevant to your life.

Many people who participate in social media have made it a rule to share few, if any, bits about their lives that aren't purely professional. They still have managed to cultivate a following by focusing on information that others find interesting and useful.

Presenting yourself online with your professional hat on not only connects you with people who are interested in the work you're sharing (and responding to it); they also become part of a support system that makes life online a little more comfortable and enjoyable. "There's an energy, a very natural way of working with social media, that reduces burnout," says Allison

Fine, author and social media consultant. "And I don't think of myself as a tech person at all, which is the beauty of working in the social media world—if you're a good sharer, a good connector, a good celebrator of other people's work, you'll be just fine in social media."[18] The more you enjoy yourself, the more productive and successful you'll be with the time you spend on social networks. The professional selves we use on social networks should by no means be stuffy or loaded with organizational-speak, and relaxed conversations having insight and expertise bring renewed spirit to the work we do.

A professional style of online interaction works particularly well for folks concerned about privacy. You can participate fully without feeling as though your life is an open book, and you'll be sharing your insight and ideas in important forums. Here are some people I follow on Twitter who contribute smart insights and personality without getting personal:

- **Lynne d Johnson**, @lynneluvah, is senior vice president of social media at the Advertising Research Foundation. You'll find her talking technology, business applications, pop culture and music, as well as some politics.

- **Johanna Vondeling**, @jvondeling, is the editor of this here book and vice president of editorial and digital at Berrett-Koehler Publishers. She's become a wealth of information for folks grappling with the changing nature of the publishing industry, as well as a source of good political links.

- **Rob "Biko" Baker**, @bikobaker, director of the League of Independent Voters, comments on social and electoral politics, especially as related to young people, and he discusses events in the hip-hop end of the universe.

- **Amanda Terkel**, @aterkel, deputy editor of ThinkProgress
.org, posts about progressive/liberal/Democratic politics,
with a healthy dose of D.C. attitude.

Additionally, sharing expertise allows you to develop your
"voice" over time—you don't have the pressure of showing up
with a "personality," as traditional media, or even blogging,
often demands.

So maybe you're not the type to share the moment that your
daughter took her first steps, or that you hated the movie you
just saw. That doesn't mean that you can't share opinions about
the work you're doing, or point people in your world to relevant
and interesting articles about things you feel passionate about.
And that's exactly what you should be doing—building and
developing a base of trust with your connections and networks.

I feel like I have to get everything perfect before I post online.

Oh yes, the deadly combination of perfectionism and not want-
ing to speak up unless you know everything there is to know
about your subject . . . that'll stop you from posting just about
anything. This kind of perfectionism is more common in women
than men—a 2009 study from Auburn University in Alabama
showed that 38% of the women who were surveyed didn't feel
they "met the high standards they set for themselves" at their
jobs, compared with just 24% of men.[19] Our fear of judgment
paralyzes us into spending every last ounce of brainpower on
crafting the perfect post before unleashing it onto an audience.

Newer types of social media, like Facebook and Twitter, are
much more relaxed when it comes to writing style. The medium
is not about broadcasting a message to faceless audience members, but rather about conversing with acquaintances, colleagues,
and friends. The conversational nature of social networks frees

us up to be less concerned about perfect wording and more concerned with sharing relevant information.

Depending on your networks, people may be insightful or humorous (or both), but no one is expecting you to provide a brilliant, in-depth analysis whenever you post. Another change to online culture is that people tend not to *flame* as much on social networks like Facebook and Twitter.[20] The infrequency of flaming may be because folks are likely already friends or connected in some way that makes them more respectful of each other's views. Granted, not all online conversation is the most sophisticated, well-thought-out stuff on the planet, but the personalization that happens on social networks—combined with the empathy and trust we create—can minimize the more out-there discussions. For one thing, as discussed in chapter 4, the fact that we choose to follow and friend people makes a big difference in how we interpret what's shared with us. Looking at how previous online conversations were structured—forums, e-mail lists—we didn't have much choice in whom we wanted to receive information from when discussing a particular topic. When we receive challenging information from people we've actively chosen to share with, we're likelier to think twice about jumping on them. Another theory points to our use of photos: With more of us showing ourselves (or our children or pets) online, readers are more likely to pause and remember that they're talking to someone "real" before they respond or leave a comment. The use of these authentic personal markers, says Kevin Marks, V.P. of Web Services at BT, "taps into deep mental structures that we all have to looks for faces and associate the information we receive with people we decide to trust, through what we feel about them."[21] We're able to add at least a couple of the missing physiological cues discussed in chapter 4, which builds our trust in and empathy for one another.

Additionally, many social networks have limited space for posting updates—you probably *couldn't* present an entire analysis even if you *wanted* to. Thus you can feel free to post opinions casually. If someone corrects you, it's not the end of the world. Conversations move at light speed with social media; your faux pas is past tense almost immediately. I'm not saying, though, that you should forget it: People appreciate honesty in these situations: Saying, "I didn't know that, thanks" or "Good point, I see what you mean," is actually a great way to build social capital.

I like maintaining my personal relationships, but I don't like blending the professional and personal.

Some people have a different problem when it comes to privacy on social networks: They're very convenient for maintaining relationships with friends and family, but the thought of blending personal and work worlds is overwhelming. I hear this a lot when I'm giving workshops, most often from women.

The good news is that tools are developing in a way that gives us more granular control over which people in which parts of our lives see what. The *Share This!* website (http://www.share thischange.com) has more information about how to manage settings with the current tools.

From a career perspective, pursuing a strategy of keeping your various lives separate may be detrimental in the long term. Increasingly, organizations are using social networks not just to find candidates for jobs, but also to see what potential new hires are up to on their social networks. Being absent (by hiding your entire profile from public view) seems questionable, especially for people under 40. It's like looking up a business online now and discovering it doesn't have a website. The expectation is that you can be found, somewhere, whether on a more professional social network site such as LinkedIn or the more personal Facebook.

While we need to be pragmatic and reasonable about what we share on social networks, companies and organizations are just beginning to grapple with the role that social networks will soon play in shifting their landscape. Occasionally we hear stories about employers turning down candidates based on what they saw in people's public profiles.[22] Certain things are obvious and understandable—you set fire to your apartment, and you post the going-up-in-flames photos to Facebook . . . yeah, that's going to get you in trouble. But employers who frown upon their employees' use of social media are setting themselves up for failure in a world that's becoming increasingly reliant on reputation and recommendations. A 2009 Nielsen report conducted worldwide showed that 90% of consumers, for example, trusted the recommendations made by people they knew, and that 70% trusted online reviews, concluding that reliance on word of mouth had increased significantly.[23] Job candidates who *aren't* out there sharing their expertise and building their social capital with these tools are going to fall behind in certain communication skills.

Additionally, social networks provide a window into a candidate's personality that may be more telling than what gets presented in an old-school-style interview. Employers can see who might make a great match—even, perhaps, when they aren't out looking.

That's not to say you shouldn't take any precautions, or that you shouldn't have a certain amount of awareness, as you wade into sharing more of yourself on social networks. Certainly we've all heard about someone who's been fired for blogging, or who got in trouble later for sharing too many spring break pictures on MySpace or Facebook. Those are the extreme cases, and they do occur; equally disconcerting, however, is the idea in the back of our heads that maybe we won't get a promotion because of what we've shared of our politics, or maybe we won't even be hired in the first place. Bruce Barry, author of *Speechless: The Erosion of Free Expression in the American Workplace* (Berrett-Koehler Publishers, 2007), suggests that in the long sweep of time, we'll make cultural progress, but in the short term, it's wise to act with common sense, depending on your situation. "In the United States, political opinion is not a protected class like gender, race, and religion, as it is in other countries around the world," he says. "It's not as much about the legality of what you can do online as it is about how corporations choose to regulate speech in the workplace themselves."[24] Until employers begin to understand more widely the benefits of their employees' sharing, we'll need to make some peace with the fact that each of us must make our own decisions on what to share, based on our employers' guidelines and overall organizational culture.

In the big picture, if companies expect us to hide parts of ourselves from semipublic view, it could have a chilling effect. Would LGBT lawyers have to recloset themselves to get hired by a power firm? Or would stay-at-home parents trying to reenter the workforce—most of whom are women—have to remove family photos to downplay dedication to their families? Such self-concealment would be dangerous and potentially damaging to change efforts already under way.

I advise those who feel comfortable blending the professional and personal to Go For It. I'm asking all of you to make a pledge together on this: Share your stories and your experiences. Tell others about yourself. For millennia now, many of us have had our stories misrepresented and marginalized. We've been told that our histories don't count. We have not been visible enough to make our stories part of the larger cultural narrative. And without visibility, we are not valued. If we're not heard, we can't make a difference.

This kind of change is not going to happen overnight; we have to commit to being in it for the long haul. By starting now (or continuing where the consciousness-raising of earlier decades left off), we are creating the space for younger generations to follow.

The Benefits Far Outweigh the Hard Parts

Social networks make it easier to connect with other people around hot-button issues, but we must all recognize the trap doors that keep us from sharing fully. By being conscious of and confronting directly the bias and fears we bring to the table, we create the possibility for overlapping conversations across traditional social boundaries, cross-pollination of ideas, and the support we all need to get past the moments that make us question ourselves and hesitate.

Social media also helps us to learn more about people we already know, and in doing so, it demonstrates that even if we *really* wanted to, it's nearly impossible to surround ourselves with people who think exactly like we do.

Before blogging and social networking, it also wasn't as easy to see what the opposition was up to, or even what they really thought. It's impossible to tackle deep-seated social injustices without understanding the beliefs of those who oppose fixing those injustices, and the Internet provides that opportunity. The Applied Research Center (ARC), a nonprofit racial justice organization that publishes *ColorLines* magazine,[25] gains insight from monitoring and listening to responses—both positive and negative—to their work. "In a non-web world, we can be disconnected and isolated from each other," notes ARC's executive director, Rinku Sen. "It's not that hard to do progressive racial justice work [in that context] and never have to deal with racial conservatives. It allows people to pick and choose who they deal with."[26]

Sen has also reframed how hate speech online and other attacks influence the work of ARC. For her, it's a clear lens into where she needs to focus. "It gives me some insight as to the level of emotional heat that is directed against racial justice efforts," she says. "It reveals the rhetoric and arguments that get repeated in the opposition, and it gives me new questions to ask. For example, what is so threatening to people's identities that they get so upset when we want to pass laws to make people more equal? That's just not a question I asked myself eight years ago." The cross-pollination that happens as a result of our stories' availability presents new avenues and lenses to peer through as we tackle the world around us.

In the end, humans will always gravitate toward others like them. It's a documented sociological effect called *homophily*— a fancy way of saying that birds of a feather flock together.[27] But homophily isn't the only thing out there driving our social interactions, and as social media becomes more integrated in our daily lives, we have more opportunity to explore people and settings different from what we're used to.

It's up to us as a culture to decide, then, what we do with that information. Do we dismiss people whose views are different from ours? Is that even a possibility? We are increasingly exposed to our coworkers' and neighbors' lives. We are catching tidbits, sometimes entire chunks, about them. If we read something we disagree with, do we de-friend them? Block them? Hide them in our news feeds?

No. We don't. In fact, we can commit to doing just the opposite: using these moments both to learn about the people who surround us and to gain insight into our own motivations and biases. Social media consultant Shireen Mitchell maintains that honesty will be key as we move forward. "We are *uncomfortable* about things, but we have to be honest," she notes. "This is all of our issue—and if we all take it on, that honesty creates trust."[28]

Having begun the difficult work of acknowledging our social stratification and biases, we have laid the groundwork for creating public spaces where people of diverse backgrounds can contribute experiences, share ideas and values, and stir the pot on what needs to happen next culturally. With our eyes wide open, and having confronted the fears that keep us out of the conversation, we'll find ourselves in a promising position to build trust across the digital spectrum.

CONCLUSION   What the Future Holds

∙∙∙∙∙∙∙∙∙∙∙   ∙∙∙∙∙∙∙∙∙∙∙∙∙∙∙∙∙∙∙∙∙∙∙∙∙

MANY PEOPLE love to speculate on what the next big thing is going to be, whether it's the next killer app, or service, or what have you. The tools we use will come and go; even by the time you're reading this, half the tools I mention throughout the book could be out the window. Rather than focus on what's going to replace Twitter (or what may have replaced Twitter already—hello, people of The Future!), we should tackle some of the coming concepts that will enhance our ability to create change in the world.

First, the problems of information overload detailed in the previous chapters will start to wane as two things happen: Culturally, we'll adapt a more wide-angle-lens, holistic view of our information stream; and technologically, we'll develop tools that attach relevance and meaning to the data coming at us. With nuanced, relevant info, more granular control over our own data, and a better mindset to process all of it, we'll be more equipped to share meaningful pieces of our lives and opinions.

The web is rapidly evolving from a one-dimensional platform of information, where information is passed back and forth and it's largely up to humans to determine its meaning, to a multilayered platform called the Semantic Web.[1] The semantic *what*? Let's break this down: *Semantic* pertains to "meaning," right? So, many engineers, including the guy who created the World Wide Web, Sir Tim Berners-Lee, are working on adding *meaning* to all that information out there.

For example, instead of publishing just a straight news story with a headline, a photo, and content, Semantic Web applications will be able to attach other relevant data to that story—*pointers* (a type of invisible link) to the people, places, and subjects referenced in the story, perhaps pointers to public records like Senate bills or local laws, and so on. This will all be done automatically, without the need for humans to create the links themselves.

The benefit of adding all of this relevant, relationship-oriented information is that web developers can then build applications that sift and filter according to readers' overt specifications, or based on a profile that they've filled out, or via any other of myriad ways that tech people can come up with. Not only will this help cut down the amount of noise we experience, but it will also help us to find other people who are interested in the same things we are, or who are like us in some respect.

The serendipity that creates that kind of discovery is powerful. It feeds into the very human, primal drive that often puts us into social networks to begin with: to know that we are not alone. Matched with the element of surprise, connecting and sharing with other human beings creates an experience that is unfailingly moving and often simply delightful. We remark on what a "small world" it is when we find two people in our social networks who know each other independently from us; the truth is, it *is* a small world, getting smaller with each new relationship. Imagine that feeling of serendipity applied to discovering news, actions, and social change, and sharing becomes a network of support and empathy, not to mention a whole movement.

Not long from now, web and Internet technologies will have set the stage for each of us to have more intuitive experiences as we explore our world, online and off, and fundamentally connect to each other. It will be through pure joy that we find common ground, share our experiences, and then fight the good fight together.

RESOURCES
Yeah, But ...
• • • • • • • • • • • • •

YOU'VE MADE IT this far,[1] and maybe there's still a bit of hesitation or naysaying in your head about why you don't think you'll change the world with social networking. Fear not, dear reader, I am here for you. The following are a number of questions and comments that I've received over the years in my work. By the end of this appendix, I hope to have relieved any last reservations about sharing your insight, experiences, and values with the rest of us (we need you! I'm serious!). If not, you can contact me either through the book's website (http://www.sharethis change.com/), or on Twitter at @randomdeanna.

This is all so Big Brother! The corporations/FBI/NSA/CIA are gathering tons of information about us.

The short answer: Yeah, they are.

First, unless you live in a country run by a repressive regime, and/or participating in dissent actually puts your life in danger, I would take worries about the government with a grain of salt. One of the more political acts you can do is to share your opinions and experiences. Offering up your version of events, showing people (including Them) what it's like to be in your shoes, and sharing your vision for the world can be incredibly potent acts.

As for the corporations, yes, they're collecting this stuff so that they can try to sell you things. That doesn't mean you have to buy what they peddle. And in many cases, you can adjust your privacy settings to prevent much of your information from being shared with third parties.

For further reading on privacy and social networks, check out the "Privacy" section of the Electronic Frontier Foundation's website: http://www.eff.org/issues/privacy.

These social networks are all closed systems! They belong to someone else. Why don't we all join an open source social network?

I do have a problem with the nature of each social network being its own little world, and while there's some cross-functionality, they're not playing with one another as seamlessly as many of us would like.

Think about that in comparison with e-mail: You can e-mail anyone else with an e-mail address. It doesn't matter that you're on Gmail and the other person's on Hotmail; because e-mail was developed as an open system that was not market driven, standards were developed to ensure that different systems could talk to one another.

That's not the case with social networks. If I'm only on My-Space, and you're only on Facebook, we can't interact. Additionally, if one of those services goes down or goes away, we're kinda stuck—we have to move on to another service and start all over.

I'd love it if there were a viable open source, open standard social network that everyone participated in. At the time of this writing, some are being worked on, like identi.ca, but none have reached widespread adoption rates. And most people want and need to go where their friends are already hanging out, so until there's a big push to such a service, we're stuck in walled-garden land.[2] I'll keep track of new developments at http://www.share thischange.com/, so stop in to see if something new has popped up since this book went to print.

Good journalism requires money! We can share our stories for free, sure, but the hard work must be done by professionals who are paid.

Many people are participating in discussions about the future of news media, and I suggest looking at my list of recommended websites at the link below to get into some of the bigger questions. People need to be compensated for their work, yes, and investigative journalism needs substantial resources. But the current model just isn't working, for any number of reasons, and I suspect that information in the digital age isn't going to fit into a strictly market model.

That said, I also want to stress that social networks and media should be complementary tools, part of a larger tool kit in the social change and information distribution ecosystems. There's no magic bullet here, only great opportunities to radically shift the way we've *been* doing things.

Here you'll find a list of blogs I read for insights into the future of journalism; I highly recommend each and every one: http://sharethischange.com/futureofnews.

Everything moves so fast! Just when I learn one network, a new one pops up and I have to start all over.

It's definitely a drag that new services launch all the time, and sometimes we feel pressured to keep up with the Joneses online. Pause before joining something new, and ask yourself if this service will help you to create or maintain relationships

with people you already know or want to know. Trying out new
services can be like a little adventure. Just remember that it's
OK to abandon networks that aren't serving your needs.

Each service does seem to have its own rules and grammar,
but much of what we talk about with social capital in chapter 3
applies to *all* social networks. Once you have a good grounding
there, you should be able to carry what you learn from one to
the next.

I don't have time for any of this!

Social networking, depending on your goals, doesn't
have to take up a lot of time. Many people have no-
ticed they're spending less time searching for news
because their networks cull and curate information for
them. Instead of combing through the morning paper or
Google News links, people check their social networks to find
the most current news and information that matters to them.

People have also found that using social networks actually
decreases the amount of e-mail they receive. Even though we're
mapping more relationships online, the communication tends
to stay within social networks and not creep over to e-mail. Because there's a lot of community and discussion, some people
also spend less time on e-mail listservs and groups.

Think of it as adjusting your digital info mix instead of just
adding to it.

I've been stalked before and don't want to be found easily.

This is a tough one, especially for women. First, you can take
some fundamental precautions:

* Don't give your address or phone number, even if you
  can manage your privacy settings to keep them hidden.

You also should make sure that you don't publish personal details anywhere on your blog or website.

- If you need to make some contact information available, use a different e-mail address than the one you use for personal communication, and consider setting up a Google Voice number for telephone service.[3]

- Remember, only share what you feel comfortable with. You don't have to share your location or other sensitive information to have valuable, authentic conversations with people that you *do* want to be in touch with.

If you experience harassment or threats, notify law enforcement immediately. Many local jurisdictions aren't equipped to deal with these kinds of cases; if that's the case, contact the FBI.

The best way to deal with most kinds of minor harassment, such as annoying commenters, is to ignore them, and feel free to delete responses and comments when necessary.

I like private communications that cannot be accessed by other people.

Me too! Think of social networks as extensions of your private relationships. They're there for when you want more engagement, input, or just to share a story. Remember, you should only post—and respond to or comment on—things that you're comfortable with. It's perfectly OK, for example, to respond privately when a friend or colleague posts something that you want to contribute to, but you don't want the whole world to see your contribution.

Almost everything online is forever. That's scary!

This is actually a Good Thing™. The contributions that you share with the online universe—whether personal, professional, or both—go a long way toward achieving very macro cultural goals. First, you're helping to define and document your own history; second, you're contributing to a larger compendium of what it's like to be in your shoes. You are sharing your story to benefit those who come after you.

On the micro level, when you're first getting into it, knowing that pieces of your life are lingering out there in the ether can be scary. But if you think about how many people are also contributing to that giant pool of personal information, it sort of reduces the likelihood that you'll stand out in any tremendous way. (Unless you do something *really* embarrassing . . . just kidding.)

Keep in mind that you have control over what you share, and each service's privacy settings will keep certain information from being catalogued or indexed. But remember, too, that everyone is going to have some sort of profile online, whether or not they're participating directly (simply by being part of other people's lives, you'll be referenced in one way or another), so it's best to do what you can to shape how that profile manifests.

I feel like I have nothing to add to the conversations out there. Won't I just be more "noise"? What if no one responds to what I say?

Sometimes you don't have a lot to say, and that's fine. But there's value in adding thoughts and opinions to a conversation, even if they're just supportive statements agreeing with what's been said; what can feel repetitive is often helpful for showing solidarity.

Noise is a matter of relevancy and taste; one person's noise is another person's lifeline. Even if people aren't explicitly responding to everything you post, they are taking notice, and this feeds into the ambient awareness we talked about in chapter 3. Expecting a direct response only sets you up for disappointment; you're contributing to a flow of information, not broadcasting from a remote island in the ocean.

These technologies are making everyone stupider! No one has any attention span anymore.

It's true that we're more easily distracted than ever—and in many cases, it's going to be up to us as individuals to take breaks from the flood of information available to us at all times and to resist the urge to check in every time we think of it.

On the flip side, studies have shown that a healthy amount of distraction is not bad for us—it helps our creativity to daydream and bounce around a little, rather than staying intensely focused on one task.[4]

Why should I organize online when I have so little precious time and so few money resources as it is? Doesn't this take away from the work on the ground?

A learning curve investment definitely has to be made, but realize that developing your community online is complementary to the work that you are doing offline—not replacing it. You don't have to go full force into every social network right away. If you're limited as to how much time you can put in at the beginning, Kety Esquivel, new media manager at National Council of La Raza, suggests picking one small goal, and one low-cost, easy tool to help you achieve that goal. Don't break your back to come up with an entire social media strategy and figure out how you're going to implement it—the work you do online should be considered another available tool in the tool kit, not just another task to complete.

Technology is taking over our lives! There's no such thing as (tech-) free time anymore.

I hear you on that one—I used to feel like that, too. But it's not technology that's the problem; it's the compulsive nature of our culture. Technology can't do anything on its own. The users have to change their behavior. We have the capability to draw boundaries where we don't want technology to infiltrate.

Right now, our culture's competitiveness compels us to always be on—we fear we'll miss something if we're not looking. Some jobs *do* require always-on connectivity, but most don't. It's time for a reality check and to remember that these tools are built to *enhance* your life, not ruin it.

Simply put, it's about managing expectations. If you suddenly disappear off the digital face of the earth, yes, people might come looking for you. But if you let people know that you're taking a break (which is becoming more and more common, and even expected), whether it's for the afternoon or the week, they'll know not to pester you with wall posts on your Facebook page.

RESOURCES
Tips for Individuals
• • • • • • • • • • • • • • • • • •

SO, NOW THAT YOU'VE figured out how you can change the world with what you share, you're looking for a few pointers either to get started or to finesse what you're already doing. You've come to the right place.

A Word about "Personal Branding"   **EVERYONE**
• •

Some social media advocates strongly recommend the philosophy of personal branding. The idea is that you pick a few keywords to build your expertise upon (good idea) and then center almost all of your professional activities in your social networks around those specific keywords, to the exclusion of everything else, much like selling a product (not so good).

The term *personal branding* has always made me uncomfortable, but it wasn't until I spoke with author and speaker Tara Hunt that I understood why. "People shouldn't be acting more like brands," she said. "We're *humans*! Instead of having a personal brand, why not just have a personality?"[5] I couldn't agree more. Remember that not only is sharing authentically what will win people over to your charming personality, but it's also what's going to change the world. Do we want to create "brands" out of each other or share our true selves?

That said, it's certainly OK to pick the areas of expertise that you want to focus on to build your professional presence—just make sure it's *you* that you're sharing, not a branded version of you.

Nuts and Bolts: Getting Started

BEGINNER

If you haven't waded too far into social networking yet, and you don't feel like you know which end is up, read on to start learning the ropes.

"Excuse me, where are the restrooms?"

One challenge of this social networking journey is that each service seems to have its own lingo and customs. Depending on the service, it can be like visiting a foreign country where you don't know the language or attending a party where you understand what's being said but you don't recognize any of the guests.

First thing upon arrival, take a look at your surroundings. Normally in these awkward situations, you might focus on finding the bar, the bathrooms, and the exit. I've got an easier assignment. Look around and ask yourself: How do I create a personal profile? How do I manage the privacy settings? What happens to my information if I want to close the account?

Finding Your People

Once you've got the basics down, it's time to start finding your people. Almost every social network has a "find friends" feature. You can enter your Gmail, Hotmail, AOL, or Yahoo address, and it will search your address book/contacts list to see if it finds

SOME BASIC PHRASINGS FOR TWITTER

- **The @ symbol.** Put this before any other Twitterer's username when you refer to the person. Why? It automatically creates a link to the person's profile, which is handy for tracking conversations or directing readers to the person referenced. It also alerts people that they've been mentioned.

- **The # symbol.** Words that follow # in Twitter are called *hashtags*. It's a way of assigning a keyword to a tweet so that others can follow the topic. You do this to make it easy to search for terms or to track popular topics (called *trending topics* or *trending hashtags*). There are myriad other uses for hashtags, but those are the basics. For an excellent and very funny video that talks about the power of hashtags, check out Baratunde Thurston's *There's a #Hashtag for That* (http://sharethischange.com/baratunde).

- **RT or rt.** These stand for *retweet*. This is a quick way of passing on someone else's post, aka *tweet*. People put *RT* and then the person's Twitter name before the tweet to indicate that it's not an original and they're just passing something along. Some people also use *via* to paraphrase. Twitter has its own retweet function, but at the time of this writing, many people find it unsatisfactory, though it's gaining in popularity.

anyone who's already a member. If there's a match, you can then choose if you want to friend or follow that person. Or if it's crazy Uncle Herb, whom you've been avoiding, you can pretend you never saw him.

The second step almost always inquires if you want to invite the billion other people in your contact list who aren't already members—please don't do this! Many of your contacts will consider it spam.

If you don't have one of the e-mail addresses associated with the service you're signing up for, that's easy to remedy— just sign up with one of those listed above for the purpose of accessing the address book. The easiest to navigate is probably Gmail; export the address book from your current e-mail program, and then import it into the Gmail Contacts list.

You can also find new friends using the info in "How to Find New Friends and Followers," in this section.

TIP: Don't be afraid to stop following someone on Twitter, or to hide someone from your feeds on Facebook or other social sites if that person's output creates unmanageable information overload. Social networks are much more flexible in their expectations of who's doing what, and you shouldn't be afraid that people will get mad if you're not reading every word they've written.

Consider looking for people you don't already know but whom you might find interesting. The most effective way is often the organic way: Watch who your friends are talking to. Click those names and scan through their posts. Find them interesting? Add them as a friend or follow them.

People Finding You

"But how will others know if I'm in their social networks?"

Well, you can start by telling them. You could go old school and send an e-mail to people you think might be interested, though not that many people do this. A subtler maneuver is to add your profile's web address to your e-mail signature. This way, you can announce it without making an announcement. Note that people you choose to follow or friend likely have their profiles set to alert them every time someone new follows them or adds them as a friend, so you don't have to tell them.

It's a good idea to use your full name in your profile so that people who are searching for you, or who have you as an e-mail contact, will be able to find you.

Another good idea is to personalize your icon or profile picture. It will help differentiate your posts in your friends' and followers' feeds, and it'll help people recognize you when they're searching for contacts. Many people advocate using a photo, but I say as long as it's something interesting and unique, go for it. My friend Tanya Tarr (on Twitter: @nerdette) has a picture of her red cowboy boots as her icon, and everyone knows it's her when she's posting.

One Big Point

BEGINNER

If you're new, it's important to realize that these networks take a while to get the hang of. You're not going to become an instant fast-moving fish swimming upstream. Commit, if you can, to trying a new service a couple of times a day for two weeks or so. At the end of your little trial period, assess how you feel and how you think you'll use it.

Use the Buddy System

BEGINNER

Find a friend who can hold your hand and be available to answer questions when you get stuck. TweetProgress.us has a list of people who have volunteered to be mentors in the progressive community (http://tweetprogress.us/users/mentors).

A Recommended Mix

- Twenty percent to 30% of what you share is about you: what you're up to, things you've accomplished, opinions you want to share, etc.

- The other 70% to 80% has nothing to do with you but is made up of things you find interesting or care about, such as links to news articles (or funny videos, even), someone else's posts that you liked, responses to and comments on others in your feed, etc.

Reputation Grooming

Your presence on social media does require a certain amount of general maintenance in order to maintain its usefulness. Spending just a little bit of time each day keeping your networks updated can go a long way toward building your social capital. It's like keeping a small garden: You pull weeds, prune good plants that have become too large, water, feed, and nurture. Oakland Local.com founder Susan Mernit refers to certain tasks we do in social networks to keep our conversations interesting and relevant as "reputation grooming."[6] Here are some maintenance items to help you grow your social media garden:

- **Setup:**
  - Make sure you complete the short bio section and add a picture for each of your social network memberships. This is very helpful for friends who are looking for you and for people who are trying to get a quick idea of your interests and types of information you share.
  - Create Google alerts for your name and/or organization and for topics that interest you (http://www.google .com/alerts).

- Save searches for relevant terms—topics you're interested in or have expertise in—in your RSS reader and/or social application. (A list of suggested applications can be found in "Applications to help you manage," later in this section.)

- **Daily routine:** Spend 20–30 minutes on the following:
  - Checking in on what's happening in your social networks.
  - Replying to comments and mentions.
  - Joining conversations on relevant topics.

- **Weekly:**
  - Check friend and follow requests, and approve/deny accordingly.
  - Check the health of your saved searches: Are they doing what you need them to do? Providing too much or too little info?
  - Check filters: Are they enough, or not enough?

- **Monthly:**
  - Weed out information sources and people who don't fit well with your stream.
  - Consider taking time to investigate new people and sources to diversify your information flow.

Dos and Don'ts   EVERYONE

- **DO** be yourself. It may be hard at first to find your voice, but you'll get there. Authenticity matters.

- **DON'T** automate your activities. Automatically following people back and sending automated private welcome messages are signals that you're in the game to collect friends and followers like bottle caps, not to have meaningful interactions. It's OK for some organizations to automate their status updates for scheduling purposes, but individuals should avoid this.

- **DO** be honest if someone is tweeting on your behalf. If you're a candidate running for office, for example, and staffers occasionally post updates, make sure the staffers identify themselves as such.

- **DON'T** use services or websites that promise to give you thousands of new friends or followers, even if they're "free." Not only is this considered spamlike behavior, but it doesn't work—remember, it's about cultivating community, not padding your numbers.

How to Find New Friends and Followers EVERYONE

- **Twitter**
  - Go to Twitter Search (http://search.twitter.com/) and enter your search terms. If you use an application to access Twitter, chances are it has a handy search function.
  - Save the search results for future use as an RSS feed[7] or with your favorite Twitter application's saved-searches function.
  - Check out the tweets of people who appear in the search results. Find them interesting? Respond to them and follow them.
  - Check back again occasionally, using your saved searches, to find more people.
  - Use the following filters to   ADVANCED   narrow your results:[8]

Location. near:city. This looks for tweets from people who have listed a city in their profile.

Example: near:Brooklyn.

Radius. within:distance. In larger cities, just putting in the city's name can return too many results, so you can add a radius to further filter it down.

Example: within:2mi.

Exclude terms. Add a minus sign before a word to find results that don't contain that word.

Example: -cupcakes.

Questions. Add a space and a question mark to find questions asked about an item or topic. Helpful for those who are looking to share expertise!

Example: lumber ?

To and from. Find tweets to or from specific users.

Example: from:maddow, to:corybooker.

- **Use BackTweets.com** to track references to URLs. This is handy for people who don't mention your name or the keywords you're tracking but who still refer to your work.

- **Facebook**
  - At the time of this writing, Facebook had announced more robust search capabilities but had implemented only a rudimentary approach. Check http://www.share thischange.com for more info.
  - People tend to use Facebook more than other services to connect with people they know. Many users make their information visible to friends only, so it's harder to determine in passing whether new people's feeds are going to be interesting if you're not already friends with them and they've chosen in their privacy settings to hide from strangers.

Managing Information Overload

EVERYONE

Yes, sometimes it seems like technology is taking over our lives and threatening our sanity. It doesn't have to! Technology is here to complement other parts of your life, not ruin them. Here are some tips for keeping it in its place.

It's not the tech, it's you

- **Information overload is not just stuff being pushed at you; it's also your own compulsion!** Technology can be like a slot machine—sometimes when you get e-mail, or check Facebook, or look at Twitter, you get rewarded with something fun. The rest of the time you don't, but you still keep trying. Be aware of that tendency to pull the lever, always hoping for triple 7s.

- **Take breaks!** It's OK to step away from your social networks and disconnect. No one will get mad at you, and if you missed anything big, you'll still find out about it. I swear.

Applications to help you manage

We were using these way back in the time and space we called 2009. For new additions, check out http://www.sharethischange.com.

- **Facebook** has mobile applications for iPhone, BlackBerry, Android.

- **TweetDeck** (Facebook and Twitter) (http://www.tweetdeck.com/).

- **Seesmic** (Facebook and Twitter) (http://seesmic.com/).

- **Twhirl** (Twitter and Friendfeed) (http://www.twhirl.org/).

- **Tweetie** (Twitter on Mac and iPhone)
  (http://www.atebits.com/tweetie-mac/).

- **AlertThingy** (Twitter, Friendfeed)
  (http://www.alertthingy.com/).

- **ÜberTwitter** (Twitter on BlackBerry)
  (http://ubertwitter.com/).

- **twidroid** (Twitter for Android) (http://twidroid.com/).

Services to help you manage

- **Ping.fm** is a website that connects all kinds of social networks together, so that you can post one update to Ping,
  and it will update all the other networks that you choose.

- **Atomkeep.com** is a service that keeps all of your social
  network profiles in sync. When you change your information (for example, jobs), you can tell it which profiles
  you'd also like to update.

E-mail is still the bane of your existence

- **Set up a different e-mail address for newsletters, action alerts,
  etc.** You should consider your regular e-mail address as a
  place for humans only, where you have contact only with
  Real People. Set up a secondary address for everything
  else, and commit to checking it as infrequently as possible.

- **Filters and rules are your friends—learn how to use them.**
  Along the lines of the previous item, chances are that at
  least some of your listserv memberships and other noti-
  fications are not providing urgent, must-read-now news.
  Use filters to automatically send them to different e-mail
  folders that you'll check periodically. Google the name of
  your e-mail program and the words *filters* and *tutorials*,

and you'll find a variety of instructional videos on how to do this.

- **Set your e-mail to manual check, including mobile devices.**
I know some of you have colleagues who will pester you and expect you to be checking e-mail every five minutes. Don't. Tell people that you're only going to be checking e-mail X number of times a day, and stick to it. Train the people around you not to expect immediate responses (by, get this, not responding immediately), and to call you for urgent matters.

- **Auto-responders: They're not just for vacations anymore!**
If you've got pressing deadlines or are otherwise going to be unavailable via e-mail, tell people with an auto-response message. Also include an approximate date when you'll be available or more responsive.

Beware the Viruses, Hoaxes, and Hacks!

Just like e-mail and websites, social networks have been targeted by malicious viruses and hacks. Often people are tricked into following links that make their accounts vulnerable, and spam is spread to their contacts through private messages and public postings.

Rule number one is to never give your password via a website or e-mail reply. Most social networks are now using authentication systems that do not need you to enter your password, except to log in to your own account. Rule number two is to use common sense. If someone in your network sends you a message like, "hey check this out i got a really cool deal" and gives you a cryptic URL, don't click it. If something about the message seems real, use another tool to contact your friend and ask if this was a valid message.

RESOURCES
Tactics for Organizations
· ·

HEY! Did you read the bit in the previous section called "Reputation Grooming"? That applies to organizations too!

List-o-Rama
· · · · · · · · · ·

Here are a few lists of reading materials to get you on your way.

- Helpful books: http://sharethischange.com/books

- People I just think are smart about this stuff: http://sharethischange.com/smarties

- Social networks for organizations: http://sharethischange.com/orgreading

- A running tally from friends and colleagues who said, "I can't believe you didn't include this in your book!": http://sharethischange.com/whoops

> **BEST SOCIAL NETWORKING QUOTE EVER**
>
> Social media is like teen sex. Everyone wants to do it. Nobody knows how. When it's done, there is surprise that it's not better.
>
> ——AVINASH KAUSHIK, ANALYTICS EVANGELIST, GOOGLE[9]

Organizations: Set Your Culture/Policy and Be Clear

Organizations need to set clear guidelines and expectations when it comes to employees' using social networks.

- Banning employees from blogging, social networking, and social media on their own time is not a good idea. However, make your group's policy clear regarding individuals' talking about their work.

- Generally speaking, businesses and organizations should encourage employees to be as open as possible, as long as it doesn't violate anyone's privacy or spill corporate secrets. Transparency is the new black.

- Also set a clear policy for employees' checking personal social network sites while they are on the clock. Obviously, employees who have more responsibility for work activities on social networks have more leeway, but all employees should be allowed time to check in.

- One note about information overload: Be very clear about your after-hours expectations. Do employees need to check work e-mail or communicate via other social networks after 5 p.m.? For some positions, this may be necessary, but remember that no one can be "on" 24/7, even though the technology is.

- Consider a tool like Yammer or   **ADVANCED** Status.net for in-house communications. They're basically Twitters for enterprise, hosted or set up on your office server, and can be completely private. Tools like these have been shown to help increase collaborative conversation and decrease long e-mail threads about project work.

Leadership Is Changing

Remember how we talked in chapter 1 about how the top-down and bottom-up organization of our culture is rapidly shifting? This also applies to organizational culture. Strong, effective leadership in this environment definitely doesn't mean rule with an iron fist, and it can be difficult to figure out how to strike a balance between collaboration and leadership. Author Allison Fine offers some tips: Bear in mind that we're all in this together, create the pathway and goals, be transparent in decision making, and develop great listening skills and flexibility.

Together, each of these tactics creates the possibility of providing guidance and a backbone for your organization, while being open to the ideas and energy that your organization and community bring to the table. Your job is no longer to be the end-all-be-all—it's to set goals and create the space for the organization to achieve them, often in uncharted territory. You'll be able to do this only if you make your group part of the process and help your group to understand why you're doing things a certain way. You'll also need to listen to their responses.

For a more in-depth look at open leadership, check out Fine's book, cowritten with nonprofit tech blogger Beth Kanter, *The Networked Nonprofit: Using Social Media to Power Social Networks for Change* (Jossey-Bass, 2010).

Social Networks Are Not ATMs

While the mechanisms of fund-raising have gotten easier—think of "Donate now" buttons and online event organizing—the actual process of fund-raising is very much the same. You can't simply roll into Facebook and start asking people for money, as much as you'd like to. In fact, acting that way would be a huge turnoff for most of your constituents and members. It's the equivalent of walking into a party, getting up on a chair, and asking everyone in the room to please give you some money because you're a very good, responsible person doing excellent things in the world. As Betsy Harman, a fund-raising strategist for nonprofits, has said, "It's still all about building relationships, telling your story, and taking potential donors through the process of cultivation, stewardship and solicitation."[10]

> In a survey published in March 2009, the Nonprofit Social Network Survey found that while 40% of all nonprofits on Facebook had raised money there, the total amount raised for each was less than $500 (http://www.nonprofitsocialnetworksurvey.com/).

Private, Roll-Your-Own vs. Joining Public Networks

In most cases, you're going to want to follow the "Go where your people are" rule of thumb and do your constituent organizing where people are already congregating.

That said, there are some advantages to using custom social networks, especially ones that are easy (technologically) to build using preexisting services. One such example is Ning .com, a community forum with blogs and video that can be made

> **RECRUITING VOICES FROM OUTSIDE YOUR OWN SPHERE**
>
> For organizations, pathways that open up to new, diverse audiences are some of the great benefits of social networks and media. It's important, once you get going, to start identifying the people who have chosen to be the ambassadors we spoke of in chapter 5. Those are the people who will be essential in helping you reach out into communities that you want to work with but haven't, due to geography or social challenges. Ask ambassadors not just for help in making connections, but also for advice on how best to make an entrance. Make sure you're not charging in as the all-knowing organization, but rather as a facilitator for change who's ready to listen.

public or private. The benefits include flexibility in creating a private/safe space for discussion and the ability to provide users with tools to self-organize around issues.

A good example of one of these networks is She Writes (http: //www.shewrites.com), where writers can gather and discuss all the ins and outs of writing and publishing. It acts much like other networks, where members can "friend" one another and create discussion groups, but offers the possibility for private discussion too. It also features educational webinars, which are open to everyone.

How *Not* to Respond to a Social Media Rampage

Just in case you do something really, unbelievably silly that makes a whole bunch of folks angry, I've compiled a quick list of Things *Not* to Do when the masses come storming your castle. This list is based on responses from other companies and organizations that have made these mistakes. The results, as you might imagine, were disastrous. Consider yourself warned:

- **Stay silent.** You know that you have an organizational blog, a Twitter feed, and pages on Facebook, but you ignore them. People aren't there to talk to you; they're there to wait patiently for your pearls of wisdom. Preferably wait at least 36 hours before making any kind of statement.

- **Go old school.** When you've finally got something to say, choose old PR strategies from broadcast media and apply them to social networks. Get your entire communications team to talk only to traditional media outlets that the angry mob will clearly listen to and be quieted by.

- **Make it up.** Don't have control over your inner situation, or any idea what's happening? Come up with a really flimsy excuse, like, I don't know, a "glitch." Your community, especially the sector that's raving loony, is clearly not savvy enough to understand the complicated nature of your organizational work. Don't admit, ever, that you are not 100% in control of the situation or that you've made a mistake. Ever.

You Are Not Alone!

Finding solidarity with other people can save your sanity on any day. Organizations now have the ability to seek out one another, share strategies, and compare notes— powerful building blocks for larger movement-building. Kety Esquivel, the new media manager for the National Council of La Raza (NCLR), has embraced this ethos. "We need to transcend these constructs in which each of us are in our isolated spaces," she says. "Whenever I present social media tools to our affiliates, I try to show them different Latino/a profiles or blogs that they'd recognize—it's about showing context, and that people are engaging in this space."[11] These tools make coalition building technologically far easier than ever and allow us to tackle the big cultural problems together.

Neat Petition Tool
••••••••••••••••

Want to make it super easy for people on Twitter to create and spread online petitions? Be sure to check out Jim Gilliam's act.ly, conveniently located at http://act.ly/.

In the summer of 2009, Allyson Kapin of Women Who Tech used act.ly to get the attention of Tim O'Reilly, organizer of numerous critically acclaimed tech conferences, and to ask him to include more women. Kapin reported that not only did O'Reilly respond, but other tech conference organizers also got in touch with her to ask how they could be more inclusive.[12]

Using *Causes* to Build Community
••••••••••••••••••••••••••••

A popular tool for awareness, fund-raising, and petitions on social networks is an application called Causes (http://www.causes .com/), currently available on Facebook (support for MySpace was discontinued in late 2009). It allows people to sign up in support of your campaigns, donate money, sign petitions, and recruit others to do the same.

One thing to remember is that Causes, as well as other applications and tools that plug into social networks, should not function as a replacement for traditional donor management and fund-raising tools.

You can find more on using Causes by checking out the organizational reading list in "List-o-Rama," p. 127.

ROI for Social Networks and Social Media
● ●

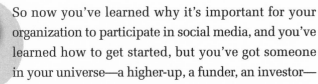

So now you've learned why it's important for your organization to participate in social media, and you've learned how to get started, but you've got someone in your universe—a higher-up, a funder, an investor—who wants to know what you're getting out of all this chitchat.

ROI (*return on investment*) typically means what kind of money you're making from all the hoo-hah, but as we've seen in other parts of this book, money and fund-raising can't be the driving forces within social networks. So let's start by reframing ROI.

Even though many of the tools used in social media are free or very inexpensive, a significant investment of staff time is still involved. That *I* in ROI means more than just how much it costs to pay for an employee to work in the social network space; it also means how much social capital you're investing in the relationships you're developing.

And the *R*, as we've said, is not just what kind of funds come out of your social network endeavors. Think of it as the relationships you're building and where you want them to lead. Remember, this is not about broadcasting and marketing; this is about engaging in two-way communication.

It's important to think about how you measure the qualitative aspects of social networks (*Do people like you? Do they respond to the work you're doing?*), and not just the quantitative ones (*How many fans do you have? How much money have you raised?*). Qualitative metrics can be tricky, but the first step is making clear decisions about what action you want your community to take.

Here are some examples:

- **Satisfaction.** Don't just look at the number of people talking about your work, but start documenting what they're saying. Is it positive? Neutral? Negative?

- **Authority.** Are they coming to your organization as a resource, looking to you for expertise?

- **Loyalty and trust.** How about repeat performance—is this their first time dealing with you? How often are they returning or interacting?

When working with these measurements, goal setting becomes crucial. It's important to keep your goals very focused, especially when you're starting out. Choose small timeframes—having X positive conversations about your work per week. Also, keep your metrics, to start, within just a couple of services. Decide that you're going to work on your Twitter presence for the next two months and then stick with it, rather than spreading yourself too thin across multiple services.

A few final thoughts to take away as you venture out into the wild world of social media ROI:

- **ROI isn't always about dollars.** It's about social capital, and the goodwill and influence you're able to work with.

- **The more specific you can get, the better.** Make your goals and corresponding metrics direct and clear.

- **Audience, audience, audience.** A reminder: This isn't a broadcast medium, it's a conversational medium. Find people who want to have the conversation with you.

- **Ditch things that don't work.** The low cost of these tools allows you to easily abandon tactics that don't work. Don't think that this means you've failed—it just means that it's time to try the next thing.

Further reading: *Social Media ROI Report: The importance of goals and success metrics*, by Peashoot, from Egg Co. (http://peashootapp.com).

The Danger of Slacktivism

For all the evangelizing we do about the power of social networks to lead to fundamental political and social change, one thing we have to keep in mind is the difference between tools that lead to offline acts of change and tools that just make us *feel* like we're making a difference.

While most of what we've covered in this book is not about taking direct action (like petitioning, phone banking, and door knocking) for advocacy, I do want to briefly discuss this as a problem to keep in mind as you move forward.

In 2009, one of the most visibly popular "actions" to take on social networks during the crisis following the Iranian elections was to turn one's photo or avatar green, the campaign color of the slightly reformist candidate, Mir-Hossein Mousavi. Within days, everyone everywhere was green (myself included) and feeling like they'd done something, when in fact Iranian activists were still being arrested, shot in the streets, and disappeared.

It's a fine line to toe, doing the hard work of raising awareness about a cause or issue (which things like colored avatars and added banners with messages do nicely) and making sure that supporters have additional, valuable actions to take. As discussed in chapter 4, we must understand clearly what these tools can and cannot do. Promoting social networks as an idealistic, magic-bullet answer for organizations engaged in activism and policy work not only is irresponsible, but also can be dangerous. Certainly the 2008 U.S. elections made it clear that plenty of activism (and fund-raising) could be conducted through social networks. What's equally important to remember is that the Obama campaign's social media tools were part of a clear, focused overall strategy that went far beyond simple awareness raising. These tools were designed to organize volunteers and to raise money in multiple ways, online and off.

Evidence suggests that group activism on social networks involving exceedingly simple, noncommittal tasks is less effective because participants aren't recognized for their work. Making it too easy to participate in a world-changing event means that people don't become emotionally invested enough to take an action that can actually make a difference. Evgeny Morozov, a Yahoo Fellow at the Institute for the Study of Diplomacy at Georgetown University and blogger at Net.Effect on Foreign Policy.com, offers excellent advice for structuring campaigns on social networks:

> So, given all this, how do we avoid "slacktivism" when designing an online campaign? First, make it hard for your supporters to become a slacktivist: don't give people their identity trophies until they have proved their worth. The merit badge should come as a result of their successful and effective contributions to your campaign rather than precede it.
>
> Second, create diverse, distinctive, and non-trivial tasks; your supporters can do more than just click [a] "send to all" button all day. Since most digital activism campaigns are bound to suffer from the problem of diffusion of responsibility, make it impossible for your supporters to fade into the crowd and "free ride" on the work of other people.[13]

Changing color may be good for raising awareness, but we need to demonstrate more than solidarity if we want to change the world. An early example of a successful campaign that engaged everyday people into taking a small but useful action was the Sunlight Foundation project "Is Congress A Family Business." Participants were asked to select a single member of

> You can use social networks to blow up issues with breaking news, but you've got to always be able to tie it back to the larger movement of what you're trying to accomplish. —KARLOS GAUNA SCHMIEDER, COMMUNICATIONS STRATEGIST, CENTER FOR MEDIA JUSTICE[14]

Congress and dig into available electoral campaign information to see if the congressperson was paying a family member from campaign funds; then they were to submit that information via a simple tool online. Organizers of the campaign kept participants and the public aware of the status of the project in two ways: (1) When a congressperson's information had been submitted, the participant was shown how many other people completed their tasks in the same time period; (2) updates were blogged on the foundation's website for the public to see.

Within two days, the information for all 435 members of the U.S. House of Representatives had been submitted, and 16 were found to be paying family members.[15] Since then, the Sunlight Foundation has led the way in creating crowd-sourced projects that are building a movement of open, transparent government.

Awareness is not enough; we must build movement infrastructure that supports full-on campaigns and utilizes social technologies to effect tangible social change.

Successful Organizations on Twitter: Wellstone Action

 The following is an interview I conducted with Elana Wolowitz, the communications director of Wellstone Action, a nonprofit organization dedicated to progressive social change, on April 6, 2009.

DZ: How long have you been on Twitter? What inspired you to join?

EW: I'm pretty sure we started in May or June of 2008. I was starting to hear more and more about the service (from bloggers and early adopters like Beth Kanter and others), and simultaneously was launching a new website for Wellstone Action that we wanted to be more interactive, and which included a blog.

I was looking for ways to be accessible to our constituents, grow our audience, and virally promote our content, so Twitter seemed like the way to go. But mostly I just wanted to try something new and experiment—throw something at the wall to see if it stuck.

DZ: Was there any organizational resistance to Twitter (or other social media)? What convinced them otherwise?

EW: I wouldn't say there was organizational resistance at all. More like organizational confusion mixed with good-natured mockery when I talked about it in staff meetings. In my role as communications director, it is in my job description to promote our work and grow our network while building our brand, so I didn't ask permission to start tweeting, and I didn't have to prove to my ED or board the value in terms of results or ROI. I said, "I don't know if this will be valuable, but it can't hurt," and any tactic that could help raise our profile was received well. After the Obama campaign, more of our staff and partners really saw the value in social networking, and then were even more on board.

DZ: Is there more than one person that tweets for your organization? If yes, how do you schedule who does what and when?

EW: Well, I am the only person that tweets from @wellstoneaction, and I also have a personal account (with much less interesting ramblings: @e_lana). Elsewhere in the organization, our training manager, Jen Haut, tweets from @campwellstone as a way to interact with participants/alumni from our flagship training program. Our executive director, Jeff Blodgett (@jeffblodgett), is on Twitter, but I am still working on showing him some of the benefits beyond just broadcasting links to our content. A few of our staff have personal accounts and mostly just "listen," but have contributed updates from out in the field—this includes Sarah Scanlon (@sarahjscanlon) and Peggy Flanagan (@peggy flanagan). Since we don't share usernames, we don't need to schedule our tweets.

DZ: What's your Twitter "plan," so to speak—what are your guidelines for tweeting?

EW: I wish I could tell you that we had a "plan"! Really, I think that the people who have said that Twitter is hard to access, but once you start doing it, you find its usefulness to you, have it right on. The only guideline I have is that our tweets should be genuine and come from a real "voice"—and that for our organizational account, that "voice" is a key part of our brand.

We try to keep it light, informal, and funny—providing helpful resources and interesting links, and being responsive to our followers, while also using it as a way to crowdsource and get buy-in and guidance on new projects. We want to have a mix of self-promotional content and links to things happening in the progressive movement that our audience should know about but might not necessarily read about from any traditional or even new media sources.

If I were to put a ratio on it, I wouldn't want to exceed 30% self-promotional content to about 70% links to other things. Some days are more on one end than others, but overall that is our goal.

DZ: What do you feel you're getting out of it? Also, are there any specific examples of a "Twitter success" that you can share?

EW: I think that the jury is still out on what we are getting out of it. Clearly there is value, but it can be hard to define. We get a direct line to our constituents, who can give us instant feedback and answers that we're looking for. It allows us to find interesting content by following like-minded organizations and partners, and pass that on, sometimes writing blog posts about things we find.

It's a good mode of communicating with the media, and we have had a couple of successes in that realm. Jason DeRusha from WCCO news in Minneapolis (@derushaj) tweeted that he was looking for sources on a story about lawn signs. At Wellstone Action, it's a running gag in our trainings that we say, "Lawn signs don't vote!" so we had a particularly interesting angle for him on the story, and I contacted him and was interviewed for the news that night. It wasn't a story I'd planned on pitching, but it was a great way to promote our brand (irreverent, not politics as usual) and help a journalist looking for a source.

Also, when Sarah Palin knocked community organizers in her speech at the RNC, we did a rapid response blog post about the real responsibilities of a community organizer. That is our only post that has gone majorly viral, getting picked up by a lot of other blogs and news sources, and Twitter helped with that a great deal.

DZ: How does it fit into your overall communications strategy? Does it ever feel like, "Oh God, I've got to tweet again," or otherwise overwhelming?

EW: It did in the beginning. I would have to get to work and sit there and think, "What the heck am I going to say today?"

I knew that I had to contribute to make it work, but was unsure what made sense. As I became more familiar with the service, and followed more people, it became easier. Twitter is a component of our overall communications strategy, but not because we have specific metrics and goals in mind. I think the medium is just too fluid for that. Right now, we're using it to grow the audience of people that are involved and help create that amorphous "buzz." Paradoxically, I think that as Twitter grows in popularity and loses some of its potency as a place for early adopters and influencers, its ability to generate buzz is reduced somewhat. But it's still a great tool in the toolbox, and I love interacting with our followers.

• • •

It's a beautiful thing to see Twitter being used organically by an organization—participating in the conversation, growing its audience and constituency through sharing of information, giving followers solid actions to take. And as a result of that organic approach, they have achieved a solid amount of success with a relatively low level of investment, when one looks at the costs of other campaign strategies. Bravo, Elana and the rest of the Wellstone Action crew!

Reprinted with permission from Care2's Frogloop, a blog about nonprofit online marketing (http://www.frogloop.com/).

RESOURCES
Crowdfunding *Share This!*

●●●●●●●●●●●●●●●●●●●●●●●●

THE PREPARATION and writing of this book was a
pretty unique experience for me that many have asked
about. The book's publisher, Berrett-Koehler, which is staffed
by some of the coolest people on the planet, doesn't offer advances to its authors. B-K feels that it's sort of like betting on
horses, and that it taints the work between publisher and author,
as well as the work that's ultimately produced. Not to say that
there aren't books that don't need large advances: There most
certainly are. But when it comes to how the market works, the
larger the advance, the greater the onus on the author to do something spectacular. And I mean that in the "spectacle" sense, not
necessarily just the "good" sense.

I decided that the book needed to be fast-tracked, given how
quickly technology changes. It would be difficult to write the
draft of a book in (what ultimately ended up being) less than four
months if I were consulting full time, so the lack of an advance
was even more complicated.

Rent needs to get paid (thanks, Hightower and Phillip, who
employ me at the *Hightower Lowdown*), and my dog, Izzy Louise,
and I have to eat. Basic principles that required me to put a price
tag on something that I feel passionate about. Weeeeeird and

uncomfortable. On top of my own expenses, I also wanted to be in a position to pay people who poured themselves into the project with me. I had originally intended only to approach foundations and large funders, looking for small grants along the way. But a couple of talks with Steve Katz and Don Hazen changed my mind.

As Steve put it—and I can't remember if these were his exact words, but this was the idea—it'd be pretty interesting to put my money where my mouth was. I'm writing specifically about the power of social media to shift perceptions and cultural values, and I'm constantly discussing new models for media and journalism with my peers. Could I leverage my social capital for this kind of good will? Also, how many people would I tick off in the process? Steve convinced me that the pros would outweigh the cons, and so far, I believe that's still true.

It was my first time doing any kind of fund-raising on this scale for one of my own projects. I'd done some arts development work back when I worked for Bowery Poetry/Bowery Arts & Science, and I'd helped out with some grant work at Alter Net.org when they were between development directors. In 2004, I worked myself into a hole of red ink, campaigning with the ABBA (Anybody But Bush Again) platform, and when I wanted to go to Ohio to work with Election Protection, I was so broke that I couldn't, as my pop says, pay attention. I sent an e-mail to all my friends, asking them to pledge money to my trip, as if it were a walkathon. That was my first experience friend raising: I raised enough money to make it to Ohio and back; even more amazingly, two friends jumped in, inspired by the e-mail, and went with me.

I returned to that format. I sent an e-mail to several hundred people in late June and of course put it out to my social networks. I set up a fund-raising page with ChipIn.com, which was free and allowed me to post a widget on my site that showed how much I'd collected.

Over the course of the summer, I was able to raise close to the amount that I needed to live on. I also received two unique donations: a monthly pizza stipend from a local eatery, and a free eye exam and new lenses from a Brooklyn optometrist. Nothing like being able to see while carb-loading and writing, says me. A family member way over in the Old Country gave me a loan for the after-book-before-work-pay-comes-in-again period. In short: I lived to tell the tale. *Publishers Weekly* even ran a story about my little adventure.[16]

Now, a couple of things I would have changed about the e-mail I sent out:

- The word *investors*, used once. Two or three people latched on to it, thinking that I was going to offer something in return for donations. I'm not. I meant *invest* in the sense of "Invest in your child's future by supporting public education" or "Invest in independent media by donating to this organization." People who donated more than $100 get a copy of the book, sort of PBS fund-raising style.

- I would have been clearer about where the money was going, that there's a whole little project happening here. I didn't want people to think it's all going to booze 'n' parties, heh. As I mentioned, I wanted to pay others who helped me, and I needed some dough for random stuff like a digital recorder (I bought a mic for my iPod in the end).

Just in case it's not been clear up to now, I don't think that this model should replace advances given to authors altogether. As I alluded to above, some authors have way bigger overheads than just me 'n' the dog. Those authors, if they do not receive advances from publishers, will need serious help from larger institutions. Crowdfunding should be one of many resources available to authors, not the sole one.

I also don't want to act as if anybody can raise $5,000 or whatever it is they need at the drop of a hat. I recognize that through my work in media, and because of the type of person I am, I've carefully cultivated an ever-growing network of fabulous, supportive people. What hasn't changed about fund-raising is that it's still about relationships. The people who work with me know that I'm there for them whenever humanly possible, and the project I'm working on will benefit our shared community at large.

This fund-raising project has been overwhelmingly emotional, in a way that I didn't expect. The people who came out of the woodwork to support this effort have given me a lot of courage to plow on with the project, and their generosity made true the ol' adage, "Do what you love and the money will follow."

Without further ado, please give a round of applause (seriously, just clap a little for them) to my wonderful donors:

Doug Kreeger	Johanna Vondeling
Don Hazen	Jaclyn Friedman
Hightower Lowdown	Tate Hausman
Ljerka Pfister	Susie Madrak
Jen Angel	Marc Faletti
Melissa Ryan	Andi Zeisler
Heather Holdridge	Erin Polgreen
Adam Green	Deb Pun Discoe
Jacki Lugg	Steve Katz
Erin Mulvey	Tracy Van Slyke
Heidi Miller	Tom Hart
Jim Gilliam	Sian Taylor Gowan
Tim Walker, Biro Creative	Phillip Smith
Two Boots Pizza	Tanya Tarr
Katherine Heald	Wendy Weidman

Paula Hasbrouck

Marc Williams

Tonya Kostenko

Elaine Lafferty

Kevin Gottesman

Brad deGraf

Sonal Bains

Julia Barry

Andrew Hoppin

Eric Squair

Elizabeth Moore

Cyn Cooley

E. J. Graff

Brave New Foundation

Philip Djwa/ Agentic

Reverend Billy and the Church
   of Life After Shopping

Jodie Tonita

Samer Rabadi

Sanford Dickert

Elizabeth Miller

Lisa Jervis

Tara Bracco

Jeff Cohen

Roz Lemieux

Amanda Marcotte

Nancy Goldstein and Joan Hilty

Bob Holman

Munn Rabôt

Gina Kim

Boyd Group Solutions LLC

David Cohn

Sam Dorman

Valentine Junker

Liz Mullaney

Nicola Wells

Sasha Forte

Brooklyn Eyeworks

Womyn's Rooms

Notes &  Treats

• • • • • • •   • • • • • •

FOR READERS WHO ACTUALLY LOOK BACK HERE

Preface

1. Pew Research Center, "Social Isolation and New Technology," Pew Research Center Publications, http://pewresearch.org/pubs/1398/internet-mobile-phones-impact-american-social-networks.

2. 🐰 The number 42 is the answer to the meaning of life, according to author Douglas Adams.

3. 🐰 "Pale, male, and stale" refers to the exclusion of women, people of color, and others from conversations about change, and thus the same ideas get repeated over and over. More on this in chapter 2.

Chapter One

1. 🐰 Birthday of the Internet: September 2, 1969. Fun stories in the comments on this Boing Boing post: "Happy 40th Birthday, Internet," http://boingboing.net/2009/09/02/happy-40th-birthday.html.

2. World Wide Web Consortium (W3C), "A Little History of the World Wide Web," http://www.w3.org/History.html (accessed September 15, 2009).

3. Ibid.

4. Ibid.

5. 🐰 The European Organization for Nuclear Research, in Geneva, Switzerland. The world's largest particle physics lab, it holds a large computing center where

the technology for the World Wide Web was developed by Sir Tim Berners-Lee.
http://en.wikipedia.org/wiki/CERN.

6. 🐦 The National Center for Supercomputing Applications at the University of
Illinois. It was one of the original sites of the National Science Foundation's
Supercomputer Centers Program, and offers engineers and scientists powerful
computing and expert support for their research. http://www.ncsa.illinois.edu/.

7. W3C, "A Little History of the World Wide Web."

8. Wikipedia, "The WELL," http://en.wikipedia.org/wiki/
WELL_%28virtual_community%29 (accessed September 15, 2009).

9. Wikipedia, "Blog," http://en.wikipedia.org/wiki/Blog (accessed January
22, 2010).

10. Wikipedia, "Independent Media Center," http://en.wikipedia.org/wiki/
Independent_Media_Center (accessed December 8, 2009).

11. 🐦 Full disclosure, my very good friend Larry (who taught me HTML in college)
worked there and tried to get me a job there several times. They had a pool
table and stand-up arcade games and beer in the fridge, so of course we all
wanted to work there.

12. 🐦 As in the "Six Degrees of Kevin Bacon" game, where one player names a
movie actor, and the other player has to connect that actor to Kevin Bacon
by using actors starring in common movies, within six steps, or "degrees."
Bacon himself became so fond of the game that he started a nonprofit called
SixDegrees.org that uses social networking to raise money for good causes.

13. Laura Green, "Grade-A Power Struggle," *Palm Beach Post News*, http://
www.palmbeachpost.com/news/schools/grade-a-power-struggle-34885
.html (accessed December 9, 2009).

14. "Testing Is Not Teaching!" Facebook, http://www.facebook.com/
testingisnotteaching.

15. As of the time of this writing. Last check-in on the group: January 22,
2010.

16. Malcolm Gladwell, *The Tipping Point* (New York: Little, Brown & Company, 2000), 41, 48.

17. Wikipedia, "Interpersonal ties," http://en.wikipedia.org/wiki/Strong_tie
(accessed September 15, 2009).

18. 🐦 For more information on how stories and information spread, check out
academic Henry Jenkins's very accessible work, most notably his "If It Doesn't

Spread, It's Dead" series on his blog, Confessions of an Aca-Fan, http://henry jenkins.org/2009/02/if_it_doesnt_spread_its_dead_p.html.

Chapter Two

1. Stan Schroeder, "Facebook: From 100 to 200 Million Users in 8 Months," Mashable, April 8, 2009, http://mashable.com/2009/04/08/facebook-from -100-to-200-million-users-in-8-months/ (accessed September 15, 2009).

2. Facebook, "Press Room," http://www.facebook.com/press/info.php? statistics (accessed January 22, 2010).

3. Stan Schroeder, "Stats: Flat Month for Social Media, With Some Surprises," Mashable, September 9, 2009, http://mashable.com/2009/09/ 09/stats-flat-month-social-media/ (accessed September 15, 2009).

4. ➴ Namely, middle- and upper-class straight white guys. I've got nothing against y'all—some of my best friends are straight white guys! I just want to mix things up a wee bit.

5. David McCandless, "Who Rules the Social Web?" Information is Beautiful, October 2, 2009, http://www.informationisbeautiful.net/2009/ who-rules-the-social-web/ (accessed November 29, 2009).

6. "Twitter and Status Updating, Fall 2009," Pew Internet & American Life, October 21, 2009, http://www.pewinternet.org/Reports/2009/17-Twitter -and-Status-Updating-Fall-2009.aspx?r=1 (accessed December 3, 2009).

7. LeWeb '09 Speakers, http://www.leweb.net/program/speakers (accessed December 11, 2009).

8. Clay Shirky, "Power Laws, Weblogs, and Inequality," February 8, 2003, http://www.shirky.com/writings/powerlaw_weblog.html (accessed September 15, 2009).

9. Keith Hampton, Lauren Sessions, Eun Ja Her, Lee Rainie, "Social Isolation and New Technology," Pew Internet & American Life Project, November 4, 2009, http://www.pewinternet.org/Reports/2009/18--Social-Isolation -and-New-Technology.aspx (accessed November 29, 2009).

10. John Horrigan, "Home Broadband Adoption 2009," Pew Internet & American Life Project, June 17, 2009, http://pewinternet.org/Reports/ 2009/10-Home-Broadband-Adoption-2009.aspx (accessed September 15, 2009).

11. Ibid.

12. Aaron Smith and others, "The Internet and Civic Engagement," Pew Internet & American Life Project, September 1, 2009, http://www .pewinternet.org/Reports/2009/15--The-Internet-and-Civic-Engagement .aspx?r=1 (accessed September 15, 2009).

13. Eszter Hargittai and Gina Walejko, "The Participation Divide: Content Creation and Sharing in the Digital Age," *Information, Communication & Society* 11, no. 2 (March 2008), 239–56, http://www.eszter.com/ research/pubs/A23.Hargittai.Walejko-ParticipationDivide.pdf (accessed September 15, 2009).

14. Noam Cohen, "Wikipedia Looks Hard at Its Culture," *New York Times*, August 30, 2009, http://www.nytimes.com/2009/08/31/business/ media/31link.html (accessed September 15, 2009).

15. See note 4.

16. ➜ To quote Jerry Seinfeld, not that there's anything wrong with them.

17. Patrick McGeehan and Mathew R. Warren, "Job Losses Show Wider Racial Gap in New York," *New York Times*, July 12, 2009, http://www .nytimes.com/2009/07/13/nyregion/13unemployment.html (accessed December 13, 2009).

18. "2008 Hate Crime Statistics," Federal Bureau of Investigation, Uniform Crime Reporting Program, http://www.fbi.gov/ucr/hc2008/data/ table_01.html.

19. "US: Soaring Rates of Rape and Violence Against Women," Human Rights Watch, December 18, 2009, http://www.hrw.org/en/news/2008/ 12/18/us-soaring-rates-rape-and-violence-against-women (accessed December 13, 2009).

20. Jos, "Suicide ends transgender lives too," Feministing.com, November 20, 2009, http://www.feministing.com/archives/018985.html (accessed December 13, 2009).

21. David Cay Johnston, "The Gap Between Rich and Poor Grows in the United States," *New York Times*, March 29, 2007, http://www.nytimes. com/2007/03/29/business/worldbusiness/29iht-income.4.5075504.html (accessed December 13, 2009).

22. Jason Kottke, "Gender Diversity at Web Conferences," February 27, 2007, http://www.kottke.org/07/02/gender-diversity-at-web-conferences (accessed December 11, 2009).

23. Joshua Breitbart, "How Policy Is the New Literacy," People's Production House, March 28, 2009.

24. Shireen Mitchell, interview by author, July 8, 2009.

25. Ibid.

26. Horrigan, "Home Broadband Adoption 2009."

27. Breitbart, "How Policy Is the New Literacy."

28. Brian Smith, "Public Education Needs to Embrace the Information Age," the Grio, October 13, 2009, http://www.thegrio.com/2009/10/during-my-final-year-of.php (accessed November 29, 2009).

29. Eszter Hargittai, "The Digital Reproduction of Inequality," in *Social Stratification*, edited by David Grusky (Boulder, CO: Westview Press, 2008), 936–44.

30. Breitbart, "How Policy Is the New Literacy."

31. danah boyd, "The Not-So-Hidden Politics of Class Online," Personal Democracy Forum, New York, June 30, 2009, http://www.danah.org/papers/talks/PDF2009.html (accessed September 15, 2009).

32. Ibid.

33. RapLeaf, "Friends of Men vs. Women on Social Networks," April 30, 2008, http://www.rapleaf.com/business/press_release/gender (accessed September 15, 2009).

34. Bill Heil and Mikolaj Piskorski, "New Twitter Research: Men Follow Men and Nobody Tweets," *Harvard Business Review*, June 1, 2009, http://blogs.harvardbusiness.org/cs/2009/06/new_twitter_research_men_follo.html (accessed September 15, 2009).

35. Tara Hunt, "Women, Technology and Social Capital," Women Who Tech 2007 conference, http://www.slideshare.net/missrogue/women-who-tech-presentation-women-technology-and-social-capital (accessed September 15, 2009).

36. Chris Brassington, "English Speaking Hispanics Lead in Mobile Internet Growth . . . ," *Huffington Post*, August 12, 2009, http://www.huffingtonpost.com/chris-brassington/english-speaking-hispanic_b_257312.html (accessed December 8, 2009).

37. Katrin Verclas, interview by author, September 1, 2009.

38. Daisy Hernandez, "Latino Teens Used Cell Phones and MySpace.com to Mobilize," *ColorLines*, July 1, 2006.

39. James Briggs, "Social Minus Mobile = Fail," iMedia Connection, September 1, 2009, http://www.imediaconnection.com/content/24280.asp (accessed September 15, 2009).

40. Horrigan, "Home Broadband Adoption 2009."

Chapter Three

1. Wikipedia, "Gift economy," http://en.wikipedia.org/wiki/Gift_economy (accessed September 15, 2009).

2. Wikipedia, "Open source," http://en.wikipedia.org/wiki/Open_source (accessed September 15, 2009).

3. ❧ Check out all available licenses at Creative Commons, http://creativecommons.org/.

4. Tara Hunt, "Women, Technology and Social Capital," Women Who Tech 2007 conference, http://www.slideshare.net/missrogue/women-who-tech-presentation-women-technology-and-social-capital (accessed September 15, 2009).

5. Jessica Clark, interview by author, December 1, 2009.

6. ❧ More on Independents Hall at http://www.indyhall.org/.

7. Wikipedia, "Internet Relay Chat," http://en.wikipedia.org/wiki/Internet_Relay_Chat (accessed September 15, 2009).

8. Susan Mernit, interview by author, September 14, 2009.

9. ❧ Of course, nothing's perfect.

10. Spotlight on Digital Media and Learning, "Kids' Participation in Online Interest-Based Communities Leads to Offline Civic Engagement," http://spotlight.macfound.org/btr/entry/kids_participation_online_communities_offline_civic_engagement/ (accessed December 11, 2009).

11. ❧ Internet Archive's collection of health and hygiene movies: http://www.sharethischange.com/healthhygiene.

12. ❧ I had a conversation with technology poobah and author Howard Rheingold, in which I asked him what he was optimistic about for the future. He told me that he was optimistic about pretty much nothing, but that he'd chosen to remain hopeful in general. The alternate choice was being a nihilist, and that's no good for being a productive person on the planet.

13. Clive Thompson, "Brave New World of Digital Intimacy," *New York Times*, September 5, 2008, http://www.nytimes.com/2008/09/07/ magazine/07awareness-t.html (accessed September 15, 2009).

14. ♠ I'll just say it: I freaking love these hotels. I've stayed in three or four of them, I think, and they're all just lovely with lovely people working there.

15. ♠ Burning Man is a yearly festival held in the Nevada desert where people do kooky free-livin' things. More info: http://en.wikipedia.org/wiki/Burning_Man.

16. Chip Conley, "A CEO's Dilemma: Should I Take My Burning Man Pics off Facebook?" BNet, November 3, 2009, http://www.bnet.com/ 2403-13058_23-358555.html (accessed December 8, 2009).

17. ♠ Too much information!

18. Not In Our Town's website and social network: http://www.niot.org/.

19. Karen Araiza, "Pool Boots Kids Who Might 'Change the Complexion,'" NBC Philadelphia, July 8, 2009, http://www.nbcphiladelphia.com/ news/local-beat/Pool-Boots-Kids-Who-Might-Change-the-Complexion. html (accessed September 15, 2009).

20. Elon James White, "TWiB! Quickie: 'Please don't change the complexion of our pool,'" This Week in Blackness, July 8, 2009, http://thisweek inblackness.com/2009/07/08/twib-quickie-please-dont-change-the -complexion-of-our-pool/ (accessed September 15, 2009).

21. Ludovic Blain, interview by author, December 9, 2009,

22. Bob Holman, interview by author, New York, July 20, 2009.

23. ♠ In fact, someone is! Check out Jennifer Pozner's *Reality Bites Back: The Troubling Truth About Guilty Pleasure TV* (New York: Avalon, 2010).

24. ♠ Go watch this video *right now*. I know I shouldn't tell you to put down this book, but do it. You won't regret it: http://www.sharethischange.com/wesch.

25. 25. Charles Taylor, *The Ethics of Authenticity* (Cambridge, MA: Harvard University Press, 1994).

Chapter Four

1. ♠ This is the title of a book by social media expert Seth Godin: *Everyone's an Expert (about something)*, http://sethgodin.typepad.com/seths_blog/2005/10/ the_next_free_e.html.

2. Baratunde Thurston, interview by author, August 2, 2009.

3. 🔹 Don't laugh. Some of them are very smart! But not Ted Stevens, the former U.S. senator who thinks the Internet is made up of a "series of tubes," thus allowing "Intertubes" to forever be part of the online lexicon. I feel a little sorry for him because it's clear to me what happened. He needed to be educated on how the Internet works, and someone called up the IT guy to have him explain it. The IT guy probably went through 80 other metaphors that just didn't click, probably tried to explain the concept of network design, and the only thing that stuck was the image of clicking together hamster tubes. Poor IT guy. I bet he bangs his head every time someone says "Intertubes." Which is often.

4. 🔹 Jim Hightower's claim to fame. http://jimhightower.com/jim.

5. 🔹 More on the RIAA: http://en.wikipedia.org/wiki/Recording_Industry_Association_of_America.

6. David McGuire, "Study: File-Sharing No Threat to Music Sales," *Washington Post*, March 29, 2004, http://www.washingtonpost.com/ac2/wp-dyn/A34300-2004Mar29 (accessed December 11, 2009).

7. Jeff Jarvis, "Attention + Influence do not equal Authority," BuzzMachine, December 28, 2008, http://www.buzzmachine.com/2008/12/28/attention-influence-do-not-equal-authority/ (accessed September 15, 2009).

8. Michelle Greer, "How Someone With 2000 Twitter Followers Can Be More Powerful than a Person with 25,000," Michelle's Blog, June 30, 2009, http://www.michellesblog.net/twiter/how-someone-with-2000-twitter-followers-can-be-more-powerful-than-a-person-with-25000 (accessed September 15, 2009).

9. 🔹 A great real-world example of this in action is a test that Beth Kanter, a writer and consultant on social media for nonprofits, and Geoff Livingston, cofounder of Zoetica, who does social media strategy consulting, performed to see if Beth's many casual followers were more engaged than Geoff's smaller following. Read more here: "What 100K Twitter Followers Gets You," http://geofflivingston.com/2009/11/03/what-100k-twitter-followers-gets-you/.

10. 🔹 For a great visualization tool that maps out influence by political website and topic, have a look at PoliticoSphere, http://politicosphere.net/.

11. Flickr, "Explore/About Interestingness," http://www.flickr.com/explore/interesting/ (accessed September 15, 2009).

12. ◗ If you're the leader of a social change organization and you're ready to make the leap into the brave new world of using the power of social networks to advance your mission, a great book to start with is Beth Kanter and Allison Fine's *The Networked Nonprofit* (San Francisco: Jossey-Bass, 2010).

13. Stowe Boyd, "Steve Rubel Becomes Another Attention Economist," /Message, June 12, 2007, http://www.stoweboyd.com/message/2007/ 06/steve_rubel_bec.html (accessed December 1, 2009).

14. ◗ The absence of tone and body language seems to shunt slightly annoying words straight into our reptile brains and get us all upset right away. Fascinating read, check it out: Daniel Goleman, "Flame First, Think Later: New Clues to E-Mail Misbehavior," *New York Times*, February 20, 2007, http://www.nytimes. com/2007/02/20/health/psychology/20essa.html.

15. ◗ Remember when a "breaking news" bulletin on the television news actually *meant* something?

16. Danny Sullivan, "Jeff Goldblum Is NOT Dead, Despite What Google Says," Search Engine Land, http://searchengineland.com/jeff-goldblum -is-not-dead-despite-what-google-says-21588 (accessed November 27, 2009).

17. ◗ Goldblum handily addressed the misinformation in a hilarious appearance on *The Colbert Report* a few days later: Colbert Nation, http://www.colbert nation.com/the-colbert-report-videos/220019/june-29-2009/jeff-goldblum -will-be-missed (accessed November 27, 2009).

18. ◗ The story originated with a prank website that allows anyone to plug a celebrity's name into a news story template and generate a fake news report. See "Cliff Death Hoax," Snopes.com, http://www.snopes.com/inboxer/hoaxes/ cliffdeath.asp (accessed November 27, 2009).

19. "Death of Little Mikey," Snopes.com, http://www.snopes.com/horrors/ freakish/poprocks.asp (accessed December 13, 2009).

20. Wikipedia, "Iranian presidential election, 2009," http://en.wikipedia.org/ wiki/Iranian_presidential_election,_2009 (accessed December 12, 2009).

21. "Ahmadinejad defiant on 'free' Iran poll," BBC News, June 14, 2009, http://news.bbc.co.uk/2/hi/middle_east/8099115.stm (accessed December 12, 2009).

22. Daniel Terdiman, "'#CNNFail': Twitterverse slams network's Iran absence," CNET News, June 14, 2009, http://news.cnet.com/8301-17939 _109-10264398-2.html (accessed December 12, 2009).

23.   An excellent source for deeper investigation into technology's role in the Iranian protests is a talk that Katrin Verclas, cofounder of MobileActive.org, gave for the Personal Democracy Forum network on July 9, 2009: http://personal democracy.com/audio/social-media-crisis-lessons-iran-election-aftermath -katrin-verclas-mobileactiveorg. Many thanks to Katrin for discussing these events in depth with me.

24.   Dan Gillmor, "Toward a Slow-News Movement," Mediactive, November 8, 2009, http://mediactive.com/2009/11/08/toward-a-slow-news -movement/ (accessed December 2, 2009).

25.   Christine Cupaiuolo, "New Mammogram Guidelines Are Causing Confusion, But Here's Why They Make Sense," Our Bodies Our Blog, November 18, 2009, http://www.ourbodiesourblog.org/blog/2009/11/ mammograms-guidelines-are-causing-confusion-but-they-make-sense (accessed December 11, 2009).

26.   Yeah, I said it. You can ignore some things. Many things, in fact! Read on.

27.   Want to learn more about filtering your e-mail? Watch this video tutorial I made: http://www.sharethischange.com/email.

28.   Mike Musgrove, "E-Mail Reply to All: 'Leave Me Alone,'" *Washington Post*, May 25, 2007, http://www.washingtonpost.com/wp-dyn/content/ article/2007/05/24/AR2007052402258.html (accessed December 12, 2009).

29.   If you encounter people who do this, they are loony. Walk away slowly, with no sudden movements.

Chapter Five

1.   Carolyn Kellogg, "Amazon de-ranks so-called adult books, including National Book Award winner," April 12, 2009, http://latimesblogs .latimes.com/jacketcopy/2009/04/amazon-deranks-gayfriendly-books -the-twitterverse-notices.html (accessed September 15, 2009).

2.   Rachel Deahl and Jim Milliot, "Amazon Says Glitch to Blame for 'New' Adult Policy," *Publishers Weekly*, April 12, 2009, http://www.publishers weekly.com/article/CA6651080.html (accessed September 15, 2009).

3.   The "glitch" response was a mistake on many levels. We'll talk about them more in "Resources"; also, Amazon's final answer on the de-ranking was that it made the errors while updating the catalog over the weekend. See the *Toronto*

Star's report here: Vit Wagner, "Giant Amazon error spurs PR storm," April 14, 2009, http://www.thestar.com/entertainment/Books/article/617982 (accessed September 15, 2009).

4. Jo Freeman, "The Tyranny of Structurelessness," 1970, http://www.jofreeman.com/joreen/tyranny.htm (accessed January 22, 2010).

5. ↩ Just to be clear, I believe in the power of echo chambers as one tool in an activist ecosystem. There are times when rallying the troops is absolutely necessary, and the pejorative association that some people have with "echo chamber" is a huge bummer. For more on progressive echo chambers—and how to use networked media to both strengthen and supersede them—check out the book *Beyond the Echo Chamber*, by Jessica Clark and Tracy Van Slyke (New York: New Press, 2009), http://www.beyondtheecho.net/.

6. Wikipedia, "Power law," http://en.wikipedia.org/wiki/Power_law (accessed September 15, 2009).

7. danah boyd, interview by author, August 3, 2009.

8. Cheryl Contee, interview by author, July 9, 2009.

9. ↩ I had the great fortune of receiving lists of blog posts that address the role of allies in different situations, a role that is instrumental in any kind of social justice work. That list can be found at http://sharethischange.com/ally. Many thanks to Carmen Van Kerckhove of New Demographic and Jessica Hoffman of *make/shift* for their contributions to the list.

10. ↩ You can find many good, fun quotes at http://jimhightower.com/.

11. R. Roosevelt Thomas, *Building on the Promise of Diversity: How We Can Move to the Next Level in Our Workplaces, Our Communities, and Our Society* (New York: Amacom Books, 2005), 103.

12. Jessica Hoffman, "On Prisons, Borders, Safety, and Privilege: An Open Letter to White Feminists," *make/shift* and AlterNet.org, April 4, 2008, http://www.alternet.org/reproductivejustice/81260/ (accessed September 15, 2009).

13. Barry Glassner, *The Culture of Fear* (New York: Basic Books), 60.

14. Rinku Sen, interview by author, August 13, 2009.

15. ↩ It takes a certain amount of experience and slightly thicker skin to figure out who is just giving you a hard time for the sake of giving you a hard time and who actually wants to have a productive conversation in these cases. One way to suss that out, according to Tara Hunt, author of *The Whuffie Factor*, is to ask,

"How did you come to that opinion?" You can then gauge the response without judgment, and see whether it's going to be productive. Note: People who are clearly set on provoking you or derailing normal conversation are called *trolls* and should always be ignored.

16. Tara Hunt, "Women, Technology and Social Capital."

17. Barbara Glickstein, interview by author, September 14, 2009.

18. Allison Fine, interview by author, July 15, 2009.

19. "Perfectionism hits working women," BBC News, May 28, 2009, http://news.bbc.co.uk/2/hi/8072739.stm (accessed December 8, 2009).

20. ◆ *Flaming*: As discussed in chapter 4, flaming is the act of expressing extreme negative reactions online. It's often instigated by trolls who are set off by seemingly insignificant indiscretions like typos, and who don't have much else to do with themselves.

21. Kevin Marks, "How Twitter works in theory," Epeus' epigone, August 14, 2009, http://epeus.blogspot.com/2009/03/how-twitter-works-in-theory.html (accessed December 13, 2009).

22. Kit Eaton, "If You're Applying for a Job, Censor Your Facebook Page," FastCompany.com, August 19, 2009, http://www.fastcompany.com/blog/kit-eaton/technomix/if-youre-applying-job-censor-your-facebook-page (accessed September 15, 2009).

23. Kristina Knight, "Nielsen: Personal recommendations 'most trusted,'" BizReport, July 9, 2009, http://www.bizreport.com/2009/07/nielsen_personal_recommendations_most_trusted.html (accessed December 11, 2009).

24. Bruce Barry, interview by author, December 12, 2009.

25. ◆ Full disclosure, I'm happily on the board of ARC and am a huge fan of their work.

26. Rinku Sen, interview by author, August 13, 2009.

27. Wikipedia, "Homophily," http://en.wikipedia.org/wiki/Homophily (accessed September 15, 2009).

28. Shireen Mitchell, interview by author, July 8, 2009.

Conclusion

1. Wikipedia, "Semantic Web," http://en.wikipedia.org/wiki/Semantic_Web (accessed December 2, 2009).

Resources

1. ☙ Or you've skipped ahead, you cheater.

2. ☙ A *walled garden* is a service that restricts its features and content to its own members. More: http://en.wikipedia.org/wiki/Walled_garden_%28technology %29.

3. ☙ Google Voice is a free Internet-based phone forwarding service that offers lots of features to help simplify your phone communications: http://google .com/voice/.

4. For more, check out Sam Anderson's article "In Defense of Distraction," *New York*, May 17, 2009, http://nymag.com/news/features/56793/.

5. Tara Hunt, interview by author, September 2, 2009.

6. Susan Mernit, "What is reputation grooming and how much time do you spend on it?" March 30, 2009, http://www.susanmernit.com/blog/ 2009/03/what-is-reputation-grooming-an.html (accessed September 15, 2009).

7. ☙ RSS: A format for storing online information in a way that makes that information readable by lots of different kinds of software. Many blogs and websites feature RSS feeds: constantly updated versions of the site's latest content in a form that can be read by a newsreader. If you're looking for a good newsreader, one place to start is with Google Reader (http://google.com/reader).

8. John Richardson, "Five Helpful Filters for Twitter Search," *Success Begins Today,* August 2009, http://successbeginstoday.org/wordpress/ 2009/08/five-helpful-filters-for-twitter-search/ (accessed September 15, 2009).

9. Avinash Kaushik, on Twitter, March 2, 2009, http://twitter.com/avinash kaushik/status/1270289378.

10. Beth Kanter, "Hello, Washington Post: Dollars Per Facebook Donor Is Not the Right Metric for Success," Beth's Blog, April 22, 2009, http:// beth.typepad.com/beths_blog/2009/04/hello-washington-post-dolllars -per-facebook-donor-is-not-the-right-metric-for-success.html (accessed December 13, 2009).

11. Kety Esquivel, interview by author, August 24, 2009.

12. Allyson Kapin, "Where are the Women in Tech and Social Media?" *Fast Company,* August 10, 2009, http://www.fastcompany.com/blog/ allyson-kapin/radical-tech/diversifying-your-rolodex (accessed December 13, 2009).

13. Evgeny Morozov, "From slacktivism to activism," *Foreign Policy,* September 5, 2009, http://neteffect.foreignpolicy.com/posts/2009/09/05/from_slacktivism_to_activism (accessed on September 15, 2009).

14. Karlos Gauna Schmieder, interview by author, August 19, 2009.

15. Ellen Miller, "Wow! You Finished It Already!" Sunlight Foundation, October 8, 2006, http://blog.sunlightfoundation.com/2006/10/08/wow-you-finished-it-already/.

16. Wendy Werris, "No Advance, Author Turns To Fund-raising," July 13, 2009, *Publishers Weekly,* http://www.sharethischange.com/pw.

Acknowledgments
• • • • • • • • • • • • • • • • • •

 I'VE BEEN WRITING *an Oscar speech since I was about 10 years old; I've also been compiling album liner notes, should I ever become a rock star. Finally, I can put them both to good use.*

I'd like to thank the following people:

My mom, Rachael, who I am clearly the next beta-version clone of. Your fierce support and willingness to listen and learn are unmatched by any mom, anywhere. You have given me courage and the ability to laugh at myself. And you. Because, as you know, we *are* the same person. I'm OK with that, really.

My dad and my brother, "big" Gus and "little" Gus, who almost never agree with me politically, but who have never, ever failed in their love and support for me. Our shared love of all things tech gave me the curiosity I needed to poke at the world around me and wonder how it worked, as well as wonder how I could make it better.

This book was literally a messy collection of thoughts and essays jumbled together from various parts of my brain, and it could not have turned into what it did without Christine Cupaiuolo's ever-insightful editing and ever-faithful support. She made two trips from Chicago to Brooklyn to work on the draft with me (as well as clean my refrigerator), and even got this TV dinner lover to think of Amy's Roasted Vegetable Pizza as comfort food. Her wit and spirit know no bounds.

Johanna Vondeling, my wicked-smart editor at Berrett-Koehler and the vice president of editorial and digital. Her dedication to producing my vision, her understanding and hand-holding (particularly her deft handling of temper tantrums), and her unbelievable savvy in so many realms made this process deeply satisfying and fascinating. She is a treasure to authors everywhere.

Rachel Manis, Cyn Cooley, and Sonal Bains, a trifecta of Very Good Friends, who provide Very Necessary Giggle Fits. My cousin Cheryl Zandt, who proposed the idea of doing tandem writing sessions so that both of us would commit time to finishing our books. Maria Sandomenico of Tails on the Town, who looked after Izzy Louise (and occasionally me) without hesitation, whenever she was needed. My awesome, hilarious, perceptive therapist, Terry Cramer, who talks me down from the ledge and gives me a reason to laugh while peering over it. The gang at the Peninsula in Prospect Park, aka "the island of misfit toys," whose morning antics are unmatched by any other set of crazy dog people anywhere.

Don Hazen and Steve Katz, who convinced me not only that I could write a book, but also that my community would support me doing it—and then gave me oodles of advice along the way. Phillip Frazer, Jim Hightower, and Laura Ehrlich, my cohorts at the *Hightower Lowdown*, for giving me exactly what I needed to get the job done. Everyone at the Women's Media Center for the support of the Progressive Women's Voices Program. Jessica Clark, who pitched in additional 11th-hour editing and research support. Susan Mernit for her ongoing mentorship. My author friends Tracy Van Slyke, Jaclyn Friedman, and Rinku

Sen, who reassured me at every panic-stricken juncture with, "No, no, I totally felt like that, too. It's OK."

The entire team at Berrett-Koehler, who took the words and turned them into an actual book. The design and production people, who humored my nitpickiness to no end with grace and patience: Dianne Platner, art director; Randi Hazan, cover designer; Elissa Rabellino, copyeditor; Leigh McLellan, interior designer and production manager. On the making-things-happen side, there's Jeevan Sivasubramaniam, the managing editor; Mike Crowley in sales; and Jeremy Sullivan, Katie Sheehan, David Marshall, and Bonnie Kaufman, a gang of marketing, PR, and community goodness. And of course, all of the unseen voices, movers, and shakers that put their souls into this work.

Jack: hobgoblin. It's the best I could do. Cliff and Dana from My Uncle's Place also get a shout-out. Izzy Louise, the best dog on the planet (who I'm sure can read by now), who taught me transcendence, patience, and how to keep two feet on the ground.

Finally, the giant communities I find myself a part of on the social networks I belong to. You shared so much with me as I created this book: You gave me incredible insights, introductions, laughs, and support. In short, you created this book with me. Thank you all.

Fuel for the fire provided by Carvel Flying Saucers, Gorilla Coffee of Brooklyn, Ruta Maya Coffee of Austin, Amy's Roasted Vegetable Pizza, and my dad's Slovak goulash.

Index
······

A

access to Internet. *See* Internet access

The Accidental American (Sen), 90

activism for social change, xii–xv, 39–42

consciousness-raising, 46–48

crowd-sourced projects, 137–138

diversity, 17–21

finding common ground, 87–89

fund-raising, 130

implicit biases, 83–86

information exchange, 9–12

insight, 100–102

mobile technology, 26–28

offline activism, 37–38

organization resources, 127–142

power relationships, 15–17, 39–40

risk, safety, and privacy, 90–100

slacktivism, 136–138

speed, 81–83

starting points, 87–89

structureless organizing, 83–84

act.ly, 133

age demographics, 18

AlertThingy, 125

Andreessen, Marc, 3

anonymity, 35

Applied Research Center (ARC), 100–101

Atomkeep.com, 125

attention ecosystem, 65–68, 75–76, 75–80, 103

authenticity, 37, 43–45, 50–54, 115–116, 121–122

authority

attention ecosystem, 65–68, 75–76

information management, 75–80, 103

information wildfires, 68–69

institutional, 57–59, 68, 69

news misflows, 69–73

organic, 56–57, 68, 75–80, 139

popularity versus interesting-ness, 62–65

size versus relevance, 59–62

validity and relevance, 73–74

automatic messages, 121–122

auto-responders (e-mail), 126

B

BackTweets.com, 123
Baker, Rob "Biko," 94
Barry Bruce, 99
benefits, 100–102
Berners-Lee, Tim, 104
bias, 83–86
Blain, Ludovic, 48–49
blogging, 5–6, 53
bonding capital, 25
boyd, danah, 24–25, 86
Boyd, Stowe, 67
branding, 115–116
Breitbart, Joshua, 20, 22, 23–24
bridging capital, 25
Briggs, James, 27
broadband, 17-18, 28

C

Causes, 133
celebrity, 67
cell phones. *See* mobile
    technology
child safety, 89–91
Clark, Jessica, 34
closed systems, 27–28, 108–109
common ground, 87–89
Conley, Chip, 42–43
connectors, 12–14
consciousness-raising, 46–48, 83–84
Contee, Cheryl, 87
cost, 113
Creative Commons, 30
cross-pollination exercises, 87–89
crowdfunding, 143–147
crowd-sourced projects, 137–138
Cupaiuolo, Christine, 74
custom social networks, 130–131

D

dial-up, 18, 28
digital divides, 21–23, 26
digitization, 6–7

distractions, 113
diversity
    cross-pollination exercises,
      87–89
    digital inequality, 17–26
    implicit bias, 83–86
    Internet access, 18, 21–22
    mobile technology, 26–28
    the power law, 16–17
    social stratification, 24–25
    technical literacy, 22–25

E

eavesdropping, government,
    107–108
Electronic Frontier Foundation, 108
e-mail, 76–78, 108, 110
    filters, 125–126
    privacy precautions, 111
    separate addresses, 125
empathy, 40–42, 48–49
employee policies, 128–129
Esquivel, Kety, 113, 132
expertise, 22–24, 113

F

Facebook, 15, 25, 98
    Causes, 133
    finding friends, 123
    mobile technology, 27, 124
fear of technology, 89–90
finding common ground, 87–89
Fine, Allison, 93–94, 129
flaming, 69, 96
Flickr, 64
Freeman, Jo, 84
Friedman, Jaclyn, 45
fund-raising, 130, 133

G

Gandhi, Mahatma, xvi
gatekeepers, 19
gender, 18, 25–26, 91–100

getting started. *See* starting points
gift economy, 29–35, 53
Gilliam, Jim, 133
Gladwell, Malcolm, 12–13
Glickenstein, Barbara, 92–93
going viral, 68–69
Goldman, Lisa, 10–12
Google, 58, 111, 116, 118, 120
government eavesdropping, 107–108
Greer, Michelle, 60–61

H
Hargittai, Estzer, 23
Harman, Betsy, 130
hashtags (#), 117
Hightower, Jim, 41, 57
Hightower, W. F., 88
Hillman, Alex, 34–35
hoaxes, 70–71, 126
Hoffman, Jessica, 89, 159
Holman, Bob, 51
home Internet access. *See* Internet access
HTML (Hyper Text Markup Language), 3
Hunt, Tara, 31, 92, 115

I
identi.ca, 108
identity, 35–38, 42–43
  photos, 96, 119, 120
  profiles, 112, 120
  reputation grooming, 120–121, 127
implicit bias, 83–86
income levels, 18, 21
Independent Media Center (IMC), 5–6
Independents Hall, 34–35
individual resources, 115–126
influence, 15–17
information flow, 75–80, 103
information hierarchies, 9–12

information management, 75–80, 103
information overload, 75, 124–126
information wildfires, 68–69
insight, 100–102
institutional authority, 57–60, 68, 69
interestingness, 62–65
Internet access
  broadband, 18, 21
  dial-up, 18, 28
  high-speed access, 21–22
  mobile technology, 6, 26–28
  as open system, 27–28
  technical literacy, 22–25
investigative journalism, 109
Iran protest demonstrations, 71–73, 136
"Is Congress A Family Business" project, 137–138

J
Jarvis, Jeff, 60
job seeking, 98
Johnson, Lynne d, 94
journalism, 74, 109

K
Kanter, Beth, 129, 139
Kapin, Allyson, 133
Kaushik, Avinash, 128

L
leadership, 129
LinkedIn, 98
location, 123

M
managing information flow, 75–80, 103
Marks, Kevin, 96
media literacy, 74, 109
Mernit, Susan, 37, 43, 120
misinformation, 69–73

Mitchell, Shireen, 20, 102
mobile technology, 6, 26–28, 124
mob mentality, 68–69
monthly routine, 121
Morozov, Evgeny, 137
Mosaic, 3
Murdoch, Rupert, 58
MySpace, 25, 26

N
names, 35–38, 119
narcissism, 53
Netscape, 3
The Networked Nonprofit (Fine and
   Kanter), 129
news
   information misflows, 69–73
   information wildfires, 68–69
   institutional authorities, 69
   media literacy, 74, 109
   misflows, 69–73
   slow news movement, 73
   Twitter, 71–73
   validity and relevance, 73–74
Ning.com, 130–131
noise, 112–113
symbol, 117

O
Obama, Barack, 87, 137
online ecosystem
   authenticity, 37, 43–45, 50–54,
      115–116
   gift economy, 29–35, 53
   identity, 35–38, 42–43
   political change, 39–42
   safe spaces, 48–50
open leadership, 129
open source movement, 30,
   108–109
open systems, 27–28
O'Reilly, Tim, 133
organic, 75–80

organic authority, 56–57, 68, 75–80,
   139
organization resources
   avoiding slacktivism, 136–138
   Causes, 133
   coalition building, 132–133
   crowd-sourced projects,
      137–138
   custom social networks, 130–131
   employee policies, 128–129
   finding people, 131
   fundraising, 130, 133
   how not to respond, 131–132
   in-house communications, 129
   leadership models, 129
   petition tools, 133
   ROI (return on investment),
      134–136
organizing, structureless, 83–84
Our Bodies, Our Blog, 73–74

P
personal branding, 115–116
personal markers, 96
petition tools, 133
Pew Internet and American Life
   Project, x, 28
photos, 96, 119, 120
Ping.fm, 125
pointers, 104
political activism. *See* activism for
   social change
popularity, 62–65
power relationships, 15–17, 39–40
   implicit bias, 83–86
   institutional authority, 57–59
   organic authority, 56–57
   the power law, 16–17
privacy, 43–45, 90–100, 110–111
privacy settings, 97, 108, 110–111,
   112
professional networking, 25–26
profiles, 112, 120

R

race, 17, 22–23
radius, 123
RapLeaf, 25
relationship maps, 8–9
reputation grooming, 120–121, 127
resources
    for individuals, 115–126
    for organizations, 127–142
retweet, 117
risk. *See* safe spaces
ROI (return on investment), 134–136
RT/rt (retweet), 117

S

safe spaces, 48–50
    child safety, 89–91
    precautions, 110–111
    women, 91–100
Schmieder, Karlos Guana, 138
Seesmic, 124
Semantic Web, 103–105
Sen, Rinku, 90, 101
Share This! website, 96
sharing, 1–6, 14, 120
    connectors, 12–14
    information exchange, 9–12
    social networks, 7–9
She Writes, 131
Shirky, Clay, 16, 50
shopping online, 37
silence, 132
skills, 22–24, 113
slacktivism, 136–138
slow news movement, 73
Smith, Brian, 23
social activism. *See* activism for
    social change
social capital, 31–33
Social Media ROI Report
    (Peashoot), 136
social media technology, ix–xi,
    8–9, 14

social networks, 6–9
    closed systems, 27–28, 108–109
    new services, 109–110
    stratification, 24–25
software, 30
*Speechless: The Erosion of Free
    Expression in the Workplace*
    (Barry), 99
stalking, 110–111
starting points, 87–89, 116–119.
    See also organization
    resources
    applications, 121
    finding people, 116–118,
        122–123
    managing information overload,
        124–126
    mentors, 119
    people finding you, 118–119
    reputation grooming, 120–121,
        127
    sharing mix, 120
    trial periods, 119
Status.net, 129
status quo, 19–20
Steiner, Peter, 36
strong ties, 12
structure, 83–86
structureless organizing, 83–84
Stupak, Bart, 85
Sunlight Foundation, 137–138

T

Tarr, Tanya, 119
Taylor, Charles, 54
tech-free time, 114, 124
technical literacy, 22–25, 113
technology, fear of, 89–90
telephone service, 111
Terkel, Amanda, 95
texting, 6
There's a #Hasthtag for That
    (Thurston), 117

Thomas, Roosevelt, 88
Thompson, Clive, 42
Thurston, Baratunde, 56, 117
time pressures, 110, 113, 121
The Tipping Point (Gladwell), 12–13
traditional media, 7
transparency, 128
trending topics, 117
trust, 38, 40–42, 55, 56–59
TweetDeck, 124
Tweetie, 125
Twhirl, 124
twidroid, 125
Twitter, 6, 15, 138–142
   basic phrasings, 117, 123
   filters, 123
   finding friends, 122–123
   Iran protest demonstrations,
     71–73
   mobile technology, 27
   popularity ratings, 63

U
ÜberTwitter, 125
urban legends, 70–71
Utne, Leif, 41–42

V
Van Kerckhove, Carmen, 159
Verclas, Katrin, 26–28

viruses, 126
Vondeling, Johanna, 94

W
weak ties, 12–13
web browsers, 3
Weblog, 5
weekly routine, 121
Wellstone Action, 138–142
Wesch, Michael, 52
What Would Google Do? (Jarvis), 60
White, Elon James, 47
Wikipedia, 92
Williams, Evan, 5
Winer, Dave, 5
Wolowitz, Elana, 138–142
women
   online safety, 91–95
   perfectionism, 95–97
   sharing habits, 97–100
World Wide Web
   blogging, 5–6
   dot-com boom, 4–5
   origins, 2–4
   social networks, 6
The Whuffie Factor (Hunt), 31–32

Y
Yammer, 129
Yes Means Yes! (Friedman), 45

About the Author

· · · · · · · · · · · · · · · · · · ·

DEANNA ZANDT is a media technologist and consultant to key progressive media organizations, including AlterNet and Jim Hightower's *Hightower Lowdown*, and hosts TechGrrl Tips on GRITtv with Laura Flanders. She specializes in social media and is a leading expert in women and technology. Deanna works with groups to create and implement effective Web strategies to meet organizational goals of civic engagement and empowerment, and uses her background in linguistics, advertising, telecommunications, and finance to complement her technical expertise. She has spoken at a number of conferences—including the National Conference on Media Reform; Bioneers; America's Future Now (formerly Take Back America); and Women, Action & the Media—and provides beginner and advanced workshops both online and in person.

In January 2009, Deanna was chosen as a fellow in the Progressive Women's Voices program at the Women's Media Center. She also serves as a technology advisor to a number of organizations, including Feministing; the Girls & Boys Projects; and Women, Action & the Media.

In addition to her technology work, Deanna writes and illustrates graphic stories and comics, and volunteers with dog rescue organization Rat Terrier ResQ.

About Berrett-Koehler Publishers

● ●

Berrett-Koehler is an independent publisher dedicated to an ambitious mission: Creating a World That Works for All.

We believe that to truly create a better world, action is needed at all levels—individual, organizational, and societal. At the individual level, our publications help people align their lives with their values and with their aspirations for a better world. At the organizational level, our publications promote progressive leadership and management practices, socially responsible approaches to business, and humane and effective organizations. At the societal level, our publications advance social and economic justice, shared prosperity, sustainability, and new solutions to national and global issues.

A major theme of our publications is "Opening Up New Space." They challenge conventional thinking, introduce new ideas, and foster positive change. Their common quest is changing the underlying beliefs, mindsets, and structures that keep generating the same cycles of problems, no matter who our leaders are or what improvement programs we adopt.

We strive to practice what we preach—to operate our publishing company in line with the ideas in our books. At the core of our approach is *stewardship*, which we define as a deep sense of responsibility to administer the company for the benefit of all of our "stakeholder" groups: authors, customers, employees, investors, service providers, and the communities and environment around us.

We are grateful to the thousands of readers, authors, and other friends of the company who consider themselves to be part of the "BK Community." We hope that you, too, will join us in our mission.

A BK Currents Book

This book is part of our BK Currents series. BK Currents books advance social and economic justice by exploring the critical intersections between business and society. Offering a unique combination of thoughtful analysis and progressive alternatives, BK Currents books promote positive change at the national and global levels. To find out more, visit www.bkcurrents.com.

Be Connected
• • • • • • • • • • • •

Visit Our Website
Go to www.bkconnection.com to read exclusive previews and excerpts of new books, find detailed information on all Berrett-Koehler titles and authors, browse subject-area libraries of books, and get special discounts.

Subscribe to Our Free E-Newsletter
Be the first to hear about new publications, special discount offers, exclusive articles, news about bestsellers, and more! Get on the list for our free e-newsletter by going to www.bkconnection.com.

Get Quantity Discounts
Berrett-Koehler books are available at quantity discounts for orders of ten or more copies. Please call us toll-free at (800) 929-2929 or email us at bkp.orders@aidcvt.com.

Host a Reading Group
For tips on how to form and carry on a book reading group in your workplace or community, see our website at www.bkconnection.com.

Join the BK Community
Thousands of readers of our books have become part of the "BK Community" by participating in events featuring our authors, reviewing draft manuscripts of forthcoming books, spreading the word about their favorite books, and supporting our publishing program in other ways. If you would like to join the BK Community, please contact us at bkcommunity@bkpub.com.